Developing Reading and Writing through Author Awareness

Elementary Curriculum Development Office

COLUMBUS PUBLIC SCHOOLS

Related Titles

Webbing with Literature: Creating Story Maps with Children's Books, Second Edition
Karen D'Angelo Bromley
ISBN: 0-205-16975-9

Independent Learning and Literacy: Strategies for Elementary Teachers
Patricia A. Genick
ISBN: 0-205-19806-6

The Right Book, The Right Time: Helping Children Cope
Martha C. Grindler, Beverly D. Stratton, Michael C. McKenna
ISBN: 0-205-17272-5

Poetry Across the Curriculum : An Action Guide for Elementary Teachers
Aaren Yeatts Perry
ISBN: 0-205-19807-4

Essentials of Children's Literature, Second Edition
Carl M. Tomlinson and Carol Lynch-Brown
ISBN: 0-205-16751-9

Literature-Based Reading Activities, Second Edition
Hallie Kay Yopp and Ruth Helen Yopp
ISBN: 0-205-16387-4

Developing Reading and Writing through Author Awareness
Grades 4–8

Evelyn Krieger

Allyn and Bacon
Boston   London   Toronto   Sydney   Tokyo   Singapore

Copyright © 1997 by Allyn & Bacon
A Viacom Company
Needham Heights, MA 02194

Internet: www.abacon.com
America Online: keyword: College Online

Library of Congress Cataloging-in-Publication Data

Krieger, Evelyn.
    Developing reading and writing through author awareness : grades 4–8 / Evelyn Krieger.
        p.   cm.
    Includes bibliographical references (p.   ) and index.
    ISBN 0-205-17355-1
    1. Literature--Study and teaching (Elementary) 2. Authors--Study and teaching (Elementary)   I. Title.
    LB1575.K75   1997
    378.1'98--dc20   96-24586
                                                            CIP

Printed in the United States of America

10 9 8 7 6 5 4 3 2 1   00 99 98 97 96

Credits: Page 9: From *The Hobbit.* Copyright © 1966 by J. R. R. Tolkien. Reprinted by permission of Houghton Mifflin Co. All rights reserved. Page 11: From Cynthia Voight, in Donald R. Gallo (Ed.), *Speaking for Ourselves* (Urbana, IL: NCTE, 1990), p. 217. Reprinted by permission. Page 13: From *Sweet Whispers, Brother Rush,* copyright ©1982 by Virginia Hamilton. Reprinted by permission of Philomel Books.

Credits continue on page 155, which constitutes an extension of the copyright page.

To my mother,
my first teacher

Contents

Preface

"You have to be old to be an author."—Eli, age 10

"I always forget the author's name."—Karen, age 12

"Authors are bookworms."—Sam, age 13

"You have to be very smart to be a writer."—Ann, 11

"A good author draws a picture with words."—Sara, 14

I have always been in love with words. From my first poem created at age 7, to a prize-winning short story in junior high school, to a published article in college, I have been writing for most of my life. As many writers will tell you, the best method for learning to write is to read, read, and read. I have my mother to thank for introducing me to the wonder of books.

My mother was a free-lance writer and book lover. The clicking of her Smith Corona is the sound of my childhood. My earliest memory is her reading to me from *One Thousand and One Poems for Children.* From that tattered book, I learned the rhythms of language.

Early on, I learned what writers do, where ideas come from, and how stories get published. Long before process writing and whole language were in vogue, my mother trained my ear to listen to a writer's voice, to notice how words and sentences are put together. She listened to my early attempts at short-story writing, offered suggestions, asked questions, and encouraged me to read my work aloud.

So it is no wonder that when I became a teacher, I carried my love of words into the classroom, along with the beloved stories and poems of my childhood. I began my teaching career in early elementary grades, when most children are still excited about reading and writing. A few years later, I began working as a junior high school reading specialist. Sadly, the enthusiasm for reading was missing in many of my students. Reading and writing had become chores. "Love to write? Are you crazy? Reading is boring."

Of course, most of my students were not so good at reading and writing, so one might attribute their lack of interest to this fact. Still, I was determined to find a way, not only to improve their reading and writing abilities but also to stimulate, challenge, motivate, and intrigue them as well. I did not care to stay in the classroom without seeing results. I drew on my experience as a reader, aspiring writer, teacher, researcher, and entrepreneur. I watched my students closely. I listened.

Here is my journey and all that I learned.

Acknowledgments

I would like to take this opportunity to thank the following reviewers of the manuscript for their helpful suggestions: Jakie Collier (Miami University of Ohio), Cheri Cooke (Oak-Land Junior High School, Minneapolis), and Nicole DePalma (Sterling Middle School, Quincy, MA).

Developing Reading and Writing through Author Awareness

1

The Beginning
of Author Awareness

"You mean Dr. Seuss is real?"

—Josh, age 6

I always smile while remembering Josh's big eyes as I told my first-graders about Theodor Geisel's life. At the beginning of the school year, I had taken an informal inventory of each student's literacy skills as well as language skills. I had asked: What is an author? How can one become a writer? Which authors do you like? How is a book made? What is a publisher? I understood how children learned to read, but how and when did children learn about writing and writers? In what ways, I wondered, might this affect their reading?

Each child in my class had his or her own idea about books and authors. I will never forget Steven, who thought I had written our classroom books. Then there was Ben, who had already discovered the answers to my questions. His father was a successful nonfiction writer. This boy knew all about what goes into writing a book. He wrote his own stories and wanted to "publish" them. He had a favorite author. Not surprisingly, he could already read quite well, and so could four other children in the class, but there was something different about the way this boy approached his reading. When Ben read a book he did not like, he blamed the author for its lack of interest. Ben also asked questions about what he read. At age 7, Ben was already interacting with the text, and his comprehension showed this.

The Library Gang

While teaching first grade, I led an after-school club called "The Library Gang." This was a group of fourth-, fifth-, and sixth-graders who all shared an interest in books. Each meeting began with a "book brag." The children took turns telling about what they had read that week. Next came author activities, projects, and games. No homework. No assignments. No grades—just a lot of fun with books.

That was the year E. B. White died. After listening as I read his obituary, the children's interest in his life grew. I suggested creating a tribute to display in the library. Each child volunteered for one aspect of the project: illustrating White's beloved characters, making a time line of his life, listing his publications, and selecting quotes from his letters.

Something magical happened after the project. Not only did the children want to reread *Charlotte's Web* but they also became interested in reading E. B. White's lesser known works. The autobiographical knowledge the children had gained added a new dimension to their reading. For example, Gabriela reported that White was quite shy and fearful of public speaking, even at his own award ceremony. Rachel's eyes lit up. "Just like Wilbur the pig when he won first prize at the fair!"

Making Connections

The transition from first-grade teacher to junior high school reading specialist brought new challenges. The Reading Workshop curriculum, as well as the style of the class, was in my hands. What was it these Reading Workshop students needed most? Clearly, they needed work in all areas of language arts: reading comprehension, study skills, critical thinking, vocabulary, grammar, and composition. Where should I begin? Should I concentrate most on skills or literature? How could I help them transfer what they learn in Reading Workshop to other classes?

I tried everything: crossword puzzles, newspapers, book projects, creative writing, library visits, play reading, recorded books, short stories, and comprehension exercises. As in any classroom, some lessons and projects worked, some bombed. There were shining moments and dreadful pauses. Although the students seemed to be learning, I could not rid myself of this nagging feeling that I was not reaching the real problem. No matter how hard I tried to introduce my students to good literature and improve their skills, they still were not reading on their own. What difference, I wondered, could I make if my students did not practice these skills outside the classroom? The more I thought about it, the more I realized that I had basically been "tricking" them into reading.

What troubled me most was their passivity. Seldom did they question an author's message or purpose. It was I who asked most of the questions. These students lacked a vocabulary to talk about literature, hence their responses were limited, such as, "It's good," "It's boring," or "It's suspenseful."

I bent over backward to hook them on books, but, for the most part, they selected a book by its cover or thickness. Few students could even articulate what kind of book they preferred, let alone name a favorite author. Why someone would want to write a book in the first place seemed a mystery to them.

My first reaction to cure the reading-is-boring attitude was to present fast-paced adolescent books. This rarely worked. Gradually came the realization that these remedial students lacked the tools to enjoy the books in the first place, no matter how engaging or well written the story. They continued to read passively, not noticing the author's special effects such as flashbacks, foreshadowing, interesting descriptions, similes and metaphors, character development, style, or story structure. Comprehension, after all, is discovering the structure and meaning of ideas expressed by another writer. My students were not even aware of the writer!

Brainstorm

In my continued search for stimulating stories, a new idea hit me. Perhaps my class would be interested in reading a story written by someone they really knew. Hesitantly, I turned to my own published writing. Maybe that would grab their attention.

When I passed out copies of a newspaper article I had written about my father, the kids were incredulous.

"Did you really write that? How old were you? Is it true? How did you get it published? Do you have any more stories?"

These questions led to an unplanned discussion on freelance writing. I shared with the class my aspiration to write fiction. The idea that one's written thoughts and experiences could be worth dollars impressed them.

"You could write about us!" Jose suggested.

I smiled. The thought certainly had crossed my mind. I decided to read my article aloud. The students followed along closely. Afterward, they bombarded me with questions. How many brothers and sisters did I have? Where did my dad live? Was he pleased that I had written about him? Then the discussion turned to fathers. Stephanie told the class she had not seen her father in 11 years, but was going to meet him for Christmas. Tanika talked about her new stepfather.

"Let's try something," I said. "Suppose you had a chance to write a news column about a relative or someone close to you. Who would you choose? Why? How would you begin? Let's give it a try now."

No complaints; no groans. My students wrote, and what came forth that week was some of their best writing.

Afterthoughts

Why was this lesson so successful? Was it simply a matter of high interest? I remembered my first-grader, Ben. I remembered the Library Gang. Aha! My students had made a connection with the *author* of the story. Perhaps as a result, their reading became more meaningful and my article had provided them with a model and a suggested audience for their own writing.

I wondered if I could teach my students to make this mental connection between reader and writer, to develop a sense of *who* wrote the story, *how*, and *why*. Could I teach them how an idea evolves into a published work? Could I instill in them a sense of authorship?

Taking Action

I felt I was on to something. Soon, I began exploring ways to bring the author to life, to get the students to notice a writer's special touches, to view literature as a personal creation, and to critically analyze what they read. I stopped relying on content-related questions to check comprehension and instead tried using a set of general questions relating to the structure of the text. For example, I asked them to think about how the book was put together and to identify the author's purpose.

We talked about writers writing. We met writers through interviews, pictures, biographies, and school visits. My students learned that if they enjoyed a book by a certain writer, they would probably like the writer's other books. (Of course, this is not a novel idea, but it certainly is an important step with remedial readers.)

Changes

The first and most pronounced change was a renewed interest in books and writing. What more could I ask for? The sheer act of reading and writing *more* should improve ability. Gradually, it became clear that reading comprehension was improving and not just on the literal level. This new approach did not allow for passivity, thus my students spent more time engaged rather than "being taught." Test scores improved. Students were tackling more challenging material. They developed a vocabulary to talk about an author's work. They began predicting, questioning, and reflecting during and after reading—strategies good readers use.

Spreading the Word

What began as an idea turned into a research grant, a teacher's handbook, a new curriculum, workshops, journal articles, a column, and a teaching award. Many aspects of this reader/writer connection are studied in high school literature classes. I propose that not only is this appropriate for upper-elementary and junior high school students but it serves an essential function in literacy development.

At the beginning of the school year, I give my seventh-graders this quiz. I also tell them that I hope they will raise their Author IQ while they are in my class.

AUTHOR AWARENESS QUIZ

1. Name five authors.

2. Name two mystery writers.

3. Who wrote *Charlotte's Web?*

4. What two famous books did Mark Twain write?

5. Who wrote *A Wrinkle in Time?*

6. Name an author who is also an illustrator.

7. Name two poets.

8. Who created the Ramona character?

9. Name a book that won the Newbery Medal.

10. Name an author who has written a series of books based on the same character.

11. Name a book set during a war.

12. Name an author who has written humorous books.

13. What did Robert Louis Stevenson write?

14. What famous woman writer grew up in Concord, Massachusetts?

15. What famous story did Frank Baum create?

Scoring

0–4: Run to the nearest library and start reading!
5–9: You're on the way to becoming an author expert.
10–14: A high author I.Q. Keep reading.
15: Superior author I.Q! Congratulations.

2

Reading as Writers

Eating a cookie takes on new dimensions when one is aware of the recipe...or the baker. Reading, if it is to be communication, is reading with a sense of writer.
—Suzzane L. Holt and JoAnne L. Vacca (1984)

Understanding a poem, short story, article, or novel requires the reader to reconstruct the structure and meaning of ideas expressed by another writer. As capable adult readers, we experience this interaction when we reread a confusing passage or when we are struck by the craftsmanship or beauty of the words. After reading a chapter in a novel, for example, we, as competent readers, may respond by predicting outcome and reflecting on meaning or character motivation. We may wonder, at the end of the novel, how the author's life experiences helped shape the story.

In my research with elementary and junior high school students, I found that the best readers (as defined by test scores and teacher identification) showed a high level of author awareness—that is, they interacted with a text much like a capable adult reader would. This finding is supported by the extensive research of Dr. Roger Farr (1989), professor of reading at Indiana University. Dr. Farr found that good readers engage in specific mental activities that enhance comprehension. Some of these activities include:

1. Noticing author style, bias, and intent
2. Making predictions while reading
3. Having a purpose for reading
4. Asking questions during and after reading

This is not to say that these are the only characteristics of good readers. Obviously, factors such as intelligence, family background, interest, and instruction are important, too. Developing author awareness is one technique teachers can use to enhance comprehension, interest, and writing ability in their students.

I am convinced that the more young readers can see the author's touch, the better they will comprehend, remember, and enjoy the story, which leads to interest in reading and writing. Author awareness develops gradually through direct instruction, writing, classroom discussion and activities, and exposure to a variety of books and authors.

Here is a checklist of behaviors to gauge a middle student's level of author awareness. The list of items, designed to be used at the middle school level, can also serve as instructional goals.

1. Reads for pleasure
2. Categorizes books by genre
3. Identifies authors of today and yesterday
4. States specific reasons for liking or disliking a book
5. Identifies the author's intended audience
6. Understands the author's use of characterization
7. Identifies similarities and differences in the author's works
8. Has a schema for story structure and includes this in own writing
9. Has a vocabulary to talk about writing (plot, theme, metaphor, climax)
10. Identifies the author's purpose
11. Understands what is involved in the writing process
12. Composes with a sense of reader
13. Uses literary devices in own writing
14. Relates the author's background to writings
15. Reads nonfiction with a critical eye (questions assertions, disagrees with opinions expressed, rereads for clarification)
16. Identifies the author's style
17. Imitates the author's style

Here, I have identified behaviors of good readers, but one simple fact must not be overlooked. Good readers *read*. One of the primary goals of the author awareness approach is to create excitement about writers and their books. Students need to *want* to read as much as they need to learn how to do it better. After all, what good are reading skills if children will not pick up a book on their own? So, the more ways you can get your students hooked on reading, the better.

How to Read a Book

In the publishing world, editors and writers know that they must make someone want to read a book. I once read an estimate that a typical bookstore customer gives an unfamiliar paperback novel about 30 seconds before he or she decides whether to purchase it. That is why some editors say they know from the first page if the book will sell. Perhaps you have encountered this phenomenon with your students. How many times have you heard one of them say "This is boring!" after reading just a few pages?

Parents and teachers are finding it harder to sell the idea of books to children. Youngsters are bombarded with stimuli from the electronic media: Television, movies, and computer games are fast and flashy. Add to this the fact that children today are tightly scheduled and spend less time reading in and out of school. It is no wonder that they cannot sustain interest in character development or descriptive passages. It seems as if adolescent readers are expecting a car chase on the first page.

Although I believe a writer should grab the reader's attention from page one, I also recognize that many terrific books (namely, classics) meander a bit before getting to the good stuff. Some books *are* boring. The question is: How long does a reader give an author before tossing the book aside? Each reader should have his or her own quota. My personal number is 50 pages. (Life is too short to read dull books.) My students know I am fond of the phrase "Give the author a chance." This means: Give the author some time to strut his or her stuff before you trade the book in. How much time? I think, for most students, 20 pages is reasonable. I find that reluctant readers are more apt to give a book a try when they know the have the option to bale out.

But there is a catch to the 20-page rule. For some students, the beginning of the book is the hardest. They have not had enough book experience to help them navigate through an author's subtleness, flashbacks, changing viewpoints, or other writing conventions. Not only do students expect to be engaged immediately but they expect everything to be spelled out. They will frequently complain, "I don't know what's going on."

Avid readers know that writers use a variety of techniques to begin a story. Avid readers do not expect to be told everything on page one. Avid readers mentally make predictions and ask questions. Students with a high level of author awareness not only are willing to give an author a chance but they also know *how* to get into a book.

What, then, does a teacher do with the less able readers who have trouble getting started? Here are two approaches to consider.

Give Students Fast-Paced Books That Have a Hook on Page One

Think of a book as a door a student must pass through. Your job is to find books with a wide-open door. This builds confidence, interest, and reading ability. (Remember, good readers *read.*) Once the children realize what engaging stories await them behind the open door, they are more likely to work at doors that require a key.

When I first met 13-year-old Andy, he told me that "all books are boring." What a challenge, I thought. Then I came to realize that Andy never got through the beginning of a book. His parents were always pushing classics such as *Treasure Island.* His teachers had assigned Newbery Award winners. In addition to a learning disability, Andy simply did not have the sophistication (or patience) to navigate these type of books.

I guided Andy to my special bookshelf of "Hook Books." I gave my 15-second sales pitch for Paul Zindel's *The Pigman.* Andy reluctantly began reading during our independent reading time. It was not long before a grin appeared. "Now I don't like school which is one of the reasons I suppose we got involved with this old guy we nicknamed the Pigman."

Of course, if we provide only fast-paced books that hook the reader on page one, our students will miss out on many wonderful writers, characters, and stories. How, then, can we give these inexperienced readers the key to open new doors? Let's consider the next option.

Help Students Learn How to Read a Book

"Would you walk out of a movie after five minutes because you weren't sure what was going on?" I ask my students.

"Of course not," they reply.

"Well, then, it's the same for a book. Don't abandon the writer after five pages." I repeat this notion all year long. I've even overheard my students reminding each other to "give the author a chance."

In addition to convincing youngsters to hang in there for 20 pages and giving them high-interest books, I also teach them *how* to read a book. Try this idea in your classroom.

Say to your students, "Suppose you are going to tell your friends a long story. What might you want to get across in the first few minutes of the story?" Write the students' responses on the board. You may get something like this:

- When the story happened
- Who the story is about
- Where the story takes place
- What the story is about

Tell the class that a writer has an important job to do in the first chapter. You might add these points to the list:

- Introduce the main character
- Introduce the setting
- Grab the reader's attention
- Establish conflict
- Create suspense

Let your students know that a good writer may accomplish all this in one chapter, but, at the same time, the writer must make the reader want to read on, so there will always be something left to discover. After all, the story is not supposed to be over at the end of the first chapter.

Once they understand what a writer tries to accomplish in the first chapter, the next step is to help students identify these accomplishments. I help my students prepare to read a new book by:

1. Studying the cover illustration
2. Thinking about the title
3. Reading the blurb
4. Reading the reviewers' quotes
5. Learning something about the author

Then, I remind them of my reading motto that hangs on the classroom wall:

COMPREHENSION BEGINS ON PAGE ONE.

A reader must tune-in to the very beginning in order to make sense of the rest of the book. Here is a tuning-in technique.

Copy the first sentence of a novel or short story on the board. Question the students about what information can be gleaned from just the opening line. Then ask, "What do you want to know?"

Repeat this with the next few sentences. Then ask, "What do you think the writer will be telling you next?" Have the students read on to find answers to their questions and to check predictions.

This exercise serves serveral purposes:

1. It demonstrates how some writers pack their openings with information, yet other writers are more cryptic.
2. It gives students practice in active reading strategies (inferencing, questioning, and predicting).
3. It focuses students' attention.

Great Beginnings

Another way to draw students' attention to the importance of a book's beginning is to spend time looking at famous opening lines. Challenge students to match the line to the book. Give them 15 minutes of browsing time in the library to copy examples of intriguing opening lines. (Don't forget to record the title and author!)

Use the following reproducible lessons to reinforce the power of a great beginning. (Extended teaching ideas may be found at the end of the chapter.)

Great Beginnings

A good beginning grabs the reader's attention. A good beginning is the seed from which the rest of the story grows. Here is an example of a great beginning from a famous story, *The Hobbit* by J. R. R. Tolkien. *The Hobbit* is an adventure and fantasy filled with elves, dwarves, trolls, and goblins. It was first published in England in 1937 and a year later in the United States.

J. R. R. Tolkien was a college English teacher. One summer day, as he sat at his desk correcting papers, he came across a blank page. For some strange reason, he quickly wrote this sentence: "In a hole in the ground there lived a hobbit." Mr. Tolkien made up the word *hobbit* and at that moment he wasn't even sure what one looked like!

The Hobbit became a fantastic success and today it is considered a classic. The book's charm is enhanced by Mr. Tolkien's drawings. He is also the author of another classic fantasy you may know, *The Lord of the Rings.*

Chapter 1: An Unexpected Party
In a hole in the ground there lived a hobbit. Not a nasty, dirty, wet hole, filled with the ends of worms and an oozy smell, nor yet a dry, bare, sandy hole with nothing in it to sit down on or to eat: it was a hobbit hole, and that means comfort.

1. Good readers question as they read. What questions come to mind after reading the first paragraph of *The Hobbit?*

   _____

   _____

   _____

   _____

2. Good readers make predictions as they read. What do you predict J. R. R. Tolkien may include in the next paragraph?

   _____

   _____

   _____

   _____

(continued)

Your Turn

A *fantasy* is a sort of fairy tale where both realistic and magical events happen. The characters are often make believe, such as witches and mermaids. The setting in a fantasy can be part real or all make-believe. Sometimes, an author creates another world or country. *Alice in Wonderland* is an example of a fantasy.

1. Use your imagination to brainstorm a fantasy character like the hobbit. What is its name and what does it look like?

   _____

   _____

   _____

   _____

2. Describe where this character lives.

   _____

   _____

   _____

   _____

3. Now brainstorm three possible opening sentences that will make your reader want to know more.

   a. _____

   _____

   b. _____

   _____

   c. _____

   _____

Great Beginnings

From the outside, if, say, a movie camera were focused on the writer at work, the words boring *and* dull *would spring to mind. This is, however, only true from the outside. Inside, secretly, invisibly, the right writing of a paragraph or a good telling of a story tastes like an adventure as exciting as any I've heard about, taken part in, or imagined. (Cynthia Voight, 1991)*

Cynthia Voight's first novel, *The Homecoming*, was published in 1981. She is the author of other award-winning books such as *Dicey's Song* and *Izzy, Willy-Nilly.*
Here is her opening from the novel *Solitary Blue:*

When Jeff Greene was in second grade, seven and a half years old, he got home from school one Tuesday afternoon in early March, and found a note from his mother, saying that she had gone away and would not be coming back. He could read the note all by himself:
    Dear Jeffie, …

What about this opening makes you want to continue reading?

_____

_____

Your Turn

Try writing an opening paragraph that involves a note or a letter. Remember, you don't have to know the whole story.

_____

_____

_____

_____

_____

_____

_____

Great Beginnings

Have you ever stared at a blank page while trying to think of how to begin a story or composition? All writers begin with a blank page. Some writers rewrite their opening line 10 or 20 times. A good opening may tell a person a lot or very little about the story. A good opening should pique the reader's curiosity. So, next time you sit down to read a new book, pay close attention to the very beginning. The author is setting the stage. You won't want to miss this part of the show.

Browse through the library to find five books with an interesting opening sentence. Record the sentence, book title, and author below. On a separate piece of paper, tell why you think it's a good opening.

1. _____

   _____

   _____

2. _____

   _____

   _____

3. _____

   _____

   _____

4. _____

   _____

   _____

5. _____

   _____

   _____

Great Beginnings

Here are more examples of sensational beginnings from contemporary young adult books. Perhaps they will inspire you to find out what happens next. Which openings intrigue you? Using a separate piece of paper, jot down questions that come to mind after reading the opening.

Not every thirteen-year-old girl is accused of murder, brought to trial, and found guilty. But I was such a girl and my story is worth relating even if it did happen years ago.—The True Confessions of Charlotte Doyle *by Avi*

I have always known that in another life I was—or will be—a dolphin. I'm silver and gray, the sleekest thing on fins, with a permanent smile on my face.—In Lane Three, Alex Archer *by Tessa Duder*

They say Maniac Magee was born in a dump. They say his stomach was a cereal box and his heart a sofa spring. They say he kept an eight-inch cockroach on a leash and that rats stood guard over him while he slept.—Maniac Magee *by Jerry Spinelli*

Eight hundred and fifty three horrifying things had happened to me by the time I was a teenager.—The Pigman and Me *by Paul Zindel*

The first time Teresa saw Brother was the way she would think of him ever after. Tree fell head over heels for him. It was love at first sight in a wild beating of her heart that took her breath. But it was a dark Friday three weeks later when it rained, hard and wicked, before she knew Brother Rush was a ghost. —Sweet Whispers, Brother Rush *by Virginia Hamilton*

Well, you might as well know all about me and then you'll understand how Zelda and I got involved in what happened to Miss Applebaum.—A Begonia for Miss Applebaum *by Paul Zindel*

Summer is over. I hope I never have to live through another one like it.—Four Miles to Pinecone *by Jon Hassler*

Classic Beginnings

Can you match these famous opening lines with the classic book?

1. It was the best of times, it was the worst of times.
2. All children, except one, grow up.
3. The mole had been working hard all the morning spring-cleaning his little home.
4. If you want to find Cherry-Tree Lane all you have to do is ask the policeman at the crossroads.
5. When Mary Lennox was sent to Misselthwaite Manor to live with her uncle, everybody said she was the most disagreeable looking child ever seen.
6. When Mrs. Frederick C. Little's second son was born, everybody noticed that he was not much bigger than a mouse.
7. Dorothy lived in the midst of the great Kansas prairies, with Uncle Henry, who was a farmer, and Aunt Em, who was the farmer's wife.
8. "Christmas won't be Christmas without any presents," grumbled Jo, lying on the rug.
9. One thing was certain, that the *white* kitten had had nothing to do with it:—it was the black kitten's fault entirely.
10. "Where's Papa going with that ax?" said Fern to her mother as they were setting the table for breakfast.

Stuart Little   *The Wizard of Oz*

Little Women   *Peter Pan*

A Tale of Two Cities   *Charlotte's Web*

The Secret Garden   *Alice through the Looking Glass*

Treasure Island   *The Wind in the Willows*

Mary Poppins

Novel Guide

Complete the following chart during and after reading the first chapter of your novel. Copy passages or brief notes as evidence of each category.

Title: _____

Author: _____

WRITER'S JOB	**EVIDENCE**
Introduce the main character.	
Introduce the setting.	
Grab the reader's attention.	
Establish conflict.	
Create suspense or tension, or arouse curiosity.	

The Author's Touch

What I like in a good author is not what he says, but what he whispers.
—Logan Pearsall Smith

You have seen how helping students "get into" a book and providing books with strong beginnings can motivate and engage reluctant readers. Research has demonstrated that helping students to see *how* an author structures a text can strengthen reading and writing in the content areas. I have found this to be an effective method for teaching fiction. Building a schema for various genres and more sophisticated writing techniques facilitates comprehension and enables children to enjoy books on their own.

Learning to Listen

How can we help our students to read with a sense of writer? We know that reading aloud to young children develops language skills, vocabulary, writing ability, and interest in reading. Unfortunately, reading aloud often takes a backseat in the middle school curriculum. In September, the first question my students ask is "How many book reports do we have to do?" I tell them to forget the book reports for now. First, they will learn to listen.

When I read aloud to my students, I try to help them become aware of the author's touch. I tell them what to listen for, I model metacognitive thinking (my own thoughts about the text as I read it), I point out interesting descriptions, and I continually engage them in the author's writing. The first step is to get your students involved in the story. Consider the following:

"This scene doesn't appear to be very important right now. Can you think of a reason the author put it in?"

"Mr. Zindel doesn't come right out and describe John. He lets us get to know him through his actions. Based on John's actions, what words would you use to describe his personality?"

"Wow! What a fantastic description of Gus's house. I think I'll read that part again. As I read, try using the author's words to create a mental picture of this crazy house. And for homework, I'm going to ask you to draw it."

"Why do you suppose the author decided to end the chapter here? Let's make some predictions for the next chapter. What clues has the author given us?"

Listening to stories is a pleasant experience for all students, regardless of reading level. In heterogeneous classrooms, poor readers can learn a great deal from listening to more adept students respond to literature, without feeling overwhelmed at having to read the book on their own. For many of these students, their listening comprehension still exceeds their reading ability.

My Reading Workshop classes consist of small groups of students who are always a bit skeptical when I start the year off by reading to them. They also seem relieved, as if they won't have to work. Yet, through listening, my students end up doing a great deal of thinking about literature.

Reading aloud gives students the freedom to respond to books in a natural way. By not being required to put all their thoughts on paper, they become more spontaneous and less worried about the "correct" answers. The oral questioning and discussion provide an effective and immediate assessment of literal and inferential comprehension.

Getting Hooked

The next step is to get your students involved in the story. Writer/teacher Daniel Pennac (1994) says, "Reading out loud isn't enough. You have to actually tell stories, offer your treasures, spread them out before an unknowing public. Hear ye, hear ye, come and admire a real story." Draw students in with an enticing question or a prop. For example, Before reading "The Gift of the Magi" by O. Henry, I displayed a pocket watch and fancy hair comb.

Let your enthusiasm show. Read dramatically. Stop reading at a point of high interest and make the students wait until the next class. Draw their attention to the author's "special effects." For example:

> "Now the author is using a flashback. We are going back in time to learn how Jeff first met Mark. This is what Jeff is remembering."
>
> "S. E. Hinton refers to the sunset several times in *The Outsiders*. Sometimes authors use certain symbols to give deeper meaning to the story. Can you guess what the sunset symbolizes?"

Once the students are hooked on a story, I introduce a variety of comprehension activities. Here are some examples:

1. Ask students to bring in magazine pictures that represent their impressions of the characters. Encourage students to use the descriptions in the book. Post these on a "Cast of Characters" bulletin board.
2. Have students work with partners to fill in a character chart. As the story progresses, students should continue to fill in additional information such as physical description, family background, personality, and problems.
3. With books that have several characters, play "Who Am I?" Each student pretends to be a character by presenting specific clues to the class.
4. Give students the responsibility of preparing study questions for certain chapters. Have partners make a quiz for each other.
5. Have students research the author's background. Ask them to find parallels between the author's life and the book.
6. Write three questions on the board before reading a chapter. Tell students to listen with those questions in mind. Afterwards, discuss answers or use as a writing assignment.
7. Give each student the responsibility of orally summarizing one chapter.
8. Ask students to write a title for each chapter.
9. Have students listen for unusual words and phrases the author uses. Record these on a large chart. Discuss meanings and function.
10. Have students keep a listening journal where they write down their reactions, thoughts, predictions, and questions.

By the time students reach middle school, most have decided whether or not they like to read. There is still hope for reluctant readers of this age. For these children, it is sometimes not enough just to hand them a Newbery Medal book and say, "Hey, read this. It's terrific!" Instead, we may need first to open their ears and show them how to hear what the author whispers and help them discover the power of words and images to make people laugh, cry, imagine, and ponder.

The Power of Poetry

Words have power.

Children enter the world programmed for language. Babies love the sound of their own babbling and the rhythms of Mother Goose. Children play with language: "Eenie, Meenie, Minie, Moe...," "Miss Mary Mack, Mack, Mack..." How sad to see this natural inclination fade as children get into the upper-elementary grades. I believe it can be revived through poetry—not the study of meter and meaning—but through the richness of language and the delight of discovery.

Poetry has the power to startle, humor, illuminate, and touch. As teacher and poet Paul Janeczko (1983) suggests, "Poems...should be a delicious part of the feast of literature we offer our kids, not brussels sprouts that get shoved to the side of the plate." What better way to hear what the author whispers than through poetry? Perhaps you suffer from what I call "poetry poisoning"—the overanalyzation-teacher-interpretation method of teaching poetry (only serious poetry, of course, like, "Song of Myself"). As reading or English teachers, we know we should teach poetry, but we may still have that bad taste left from our own school days. If this is the case, don't fret. Why not rediscover poetry alongside your students? Here is a painless method for bringing poetry into your classroom.

Let's Get Reacquainted

Chances are that the boys in your class may think poetry is sissy stuff. And odds are that you will receive a collective groan if you announce, "Today we're going to start a unit on poetry." So be a little sneaky. Start small. Read a poem before taking attendance—and make it a humorous one, such as Shel Silverstein's "Sick." There's nothing that breaks the ice better than a good laugh. Then say nothing more—no probing questions, no rhyming patterns. (Of course you will want to acknowledge the creator of the poem.)

Continue this for a few weeks. Read at least one poem each day. This usually takes less than a minute. At different times, simply announce, "I'd like to share this limerick with you," or "This poem reminded me of Alicia," or "Anyone who has ever been to the dentist will like this poem," or "In honor of Valentine's Day, I present this poem by..."

Read poems on topics usually not associated with poetry, such as sports or food. Leave books of poetry around the classroom, particularly the books from which you have read aloud. You will be surprised at the number of students who will sneak a peek or reread the one you just shared.

Next, give students copies of funny and interesting poems just "so you can have your own copy." Don't be surprised if your students ask if they have to memorize it. They may look at you suspiciously, as if expecting a quiz on it the next day. Remember, this is all part of the plan to reacquaint them with the joy of language they once knew.

Gradually, your students will begin to associate poetry with pleasure rather than pain. When you say, "Here's a weird poem...," they will listen with open ears because they know they will not be prodded or tested. If you get no further than this daily reading of a variety of poems, you will have accomplished more than you realize. By the end of a school year, your students will have heard 100 to 200 poems and be familiar with the names of several poets. Just hearing the language of imagery, unusual words, and interesting metaphors on a regular basis enhances a young person's own language development. If nothing else, your students will have opened their minds and hearts to poetry.

A Passion for Poetry

If poetry is not your forte, or if you feel intimidated by sharing more complex or famous poems, then you must first do your homework. Any one who teaches poetry must first read it. Fill your bookbag with a variety of anthologies, contemporary poems, children's poems, poetry by specific authors, types of poems, and thematic collections. Use only the poems that grab you or that you think will grab your students.

After you are more at home with poetry and can appreciate all its possibilities, then you are ready to move beyond just sharing the poems with your class. There are several good books on the teaching of poetry to help you along. (See lists at the end of the chapter.) Here are a few ideas I have used with middle school students.

Personal Poetry Anthology   This was a successful project at Charles E. Brown Middle School in Newton, Massachusetts. Our school librarian displayed dozens of poetry anthologies in the library. Classes visited the library and were introduced to the variety of anthologies available. Students were told simply to browse through the books to find poems they liked. Over the course of a few weeks, they were to select between 10 and 20 poems by at least three different authors to include in their personal anthologies. The poems were to be copied by hand or typed and followed by a brief explanation of why the poem was selected. An illustration, photograph, or symbol was also added. (One variation is to have students select poems on a specific theme such as war or childhood.)

Students then bound the poetry pages and designed a cover. Some teachers asked them to write an introduction. In my classes, students received a B for meeting the minimum requirements and an A for an exemplary job. Most students were enthusiastic about the project. A few hard-to-reach children really became engaged. Here is why I think this is an effective assignment.

1. Students are given the freedom to select poems that have meaning to them.
2. In order to find poems they like, students must do a lot of reading, thus encountering a variety of poets and poems.
3. Students can work independently as well as together and at their own pace.
4. There are no right or wrong answers.

Poet in the Classroom   Some schools sponsor a poet-in-residence program that brings a poet into the school for several days to conduct workshops with teachers and students. I was fortunate that the mother of one of my students was a poet and volunteered her time in our classroom. She shared her own poetry and conducted interesting exercises that unleashed the natural poet in us all.

The Music of Poetry   Have students write down the lyrics of their favorite songs. (I don't permit anything obscene or excessively violent.) Do the words stand alone? Do the lyrics make a good poem? How are songs different from poems? Which poems might make a good song? Musically inclined students may want to try this activity.

Poetry Place   Cover a wall with paper. Allow students to write their own poems, copy ones they like, and dedicate poems to their friends. Challenge them to find examples of haiku, cinquain, and acrostic poems.

Poet of the Week/Month   Feature the work of a poet such as Langston Hughes, Robert Frost, Nikki Giovanni, or Eloise Wilkin. Share stories about the poet's life and study the time period in which he or she wrote.

Lists of poetry anthologies and resources may be found at the end of this chapter. (An extended teaching idea also may be found at the end of the chapter.)

Lisa was a shy, unsocial girl who joined my seventh-grade English class in March. Her one request during our initial meeting was not to call on her to read out loud in class. I didn't mind honoring Lisa's request. I had taught other students who were self-conscious about reading aloud, and found it was best not to push. However, within a few days, I learned that Lisa would not answer any questions out loud either. Since discussion was an integral part of the literature program, Lisa was at a disadvantage. If I called on her, she would blush and shrug her shoulders, even when I was sure she knew the answer. To make matters worse, she did not turn in any written work either. She would say that she left her draft at home, lost it on the computer, or needed more time.

After a conference with Lisa's parents, as well as reading her school file, I learned that Lisa had always been a painfully shy and self-conscious child. She had recently begun counseling. I wondered if I could find a way to reach this silent student.

When I asked Lisa how I could grade her without written work or class participation, she looked confused then hurt.

"But I always do the reading," she replied in her soft voice.

"I'm glad to hear that. But writing is part of the class as well."

Lisa then told me that she didn't care for *that* kind of writing. She only liked writing in her diary. Lisa remained withdrawn during the following weeks. Yet, when we began poetry unit, I noticed that Lisa paid close attention in class. While reading Langston Hughes's poetry, I thought I saw a sparkle in her eyes. To conclude our study of his poetry, I asked the students to illustrate Hughes's famous poem "Dreams."

For the first time, Lisa outdid herself—and her classmates—with a beautiful drawing that effectively expressed Hughes's message. She was embarrassed by all the attention her drawing received from classmates and the praise I gave her. But I detected a feeling of pride as well. Perhaps, I thought, I found Lisa's niche.

During the next two weeks, the students worked on creating individual poetry anthologies, including an illustration and comment on each poem they selected. Each day, I gave the students time to work in the library. Lisa usually sat alone, flipping through poetry books, but I never saw her copy any poems in her notebook. On the day the anthologies were due, Lisa nonchalantly dropped a thick, beautifully bound book on my desk. That night, as I read her anthology, I was astonished to find that Lisa had written all 20 poems herself, each one lavishly illustrated with watercolors and pastels. She included a brief comment on why or when she had written each poem. They were all poems about love.

Though Lisa could not speak aloud to the class, she could indeed whisper through poetry. When I think about teaching students such as Lisa, I'm reminded of Langston Hughes's own description of writing poetry: "Poems are like rainbows, you have to catch them quickly, before they disappear."

Developing Author Awareness
through Effective Questioning

An effective reader is a critical reader. Critical reading requires consideration of an author's intention and an evaluation of the accuracy and quality of a text. The good reader asks, "Why is the author telling me this in this way?"

—Timothy Shanahan (1988)

Through the use of effective questioning, we can help our students develop author awareness and critical reading ability. Are discussion and after-reading questions the staple of comprehension activities in your classroom? I became frustrated by the plethora of after-reading questions designed to determine if the students had read the story or to test recall of specific details. These type of questions helped me determine whether the students understood or recalled a part of the text, but they did not permit me to see what the students had learned. Had the students' intellect and imagination really been stretched?

Give the comprehension questions you use a close examination.

1. Do they assess and instruct at the same time?
2. Do they ask students to read both literally and inferentially?
3. Do they ask students to reread passages and to support answers?
4. Do they ask students to discover the author's touch?
5. Do they allow for more than one answer?

In reading fiction, we often ask students where and when the story takes place. If this simple question is reworded as, "How does the author let you know when and where the story takes place?" the students must not only recall the setting but also think about how they came to know it. To answer the question completely, they must think, reread, and look for supporting passages. Students begin to discover a writer's methods for creating a setting. This is comprehension in action.

Creating Key Questions

When students are reading different novels, it is burdensome for the teacher to create text-specific questions. Published comprehension exercises and activities are available for specific book titles, but this can still generate a great deal of paperwork if you use an independent reading program. Upon close examination, you may find many of the questions at the literal level. Now you may be asking, "But how can I know if they read the book as well as understood it?" I solved this problem by designing a generic list of author awareness questions for student response during and after reading.

Sometimes, students find these author awareness questions too complex. They are accustomed to narrow questions with one right answer. I say, "Maybe you have never been asked to read in this way. Now that you are in seventh grade, you will be doing some sophisticated thinking." Then I elaborate on the questions and help direct students' thinking. Often, I set aside class time for working on question responses. I use these questions over and over in different ways so that students will eventually internalize them. This process leads to active reading and high-level comprehension.

Here are the questions and ways in which to use them.

AUTHOR AWARENESS QUESTIONS
FOR COMPREHENSION

Plot

- How does the author let you know where the story happens? When did you first begin to learn about the setting? Give examples of changing settings.
- Describe what you believe to be one of the most important scenes in the story.
- What questions did you have while reading? Were the questions answered by the end?
- Did the author give you any clues to the outcome?

Style

- Find (or copy) a passage in the book/story where you think the author has done a great job with description. What makes this passage good? How does it help the story?
- Copy examples of similes and metaphors that you think are good.
- How does the author create suspense or at least make you curious about what will happen?

Characterization

- Find (or copy) a passage in which the author *shows* you a character's personality. Then find one in which the author *tells* you about character's personality.
- Find (or copy) a passage of dialogue that tells you something important about a character. Explain why it is important.
- In what ways do the characters change in the book? How does the author help you to notice these changes?
- After reading the story, which character do you feel you know best? How did the author help you to know so much about this character?

Structure

- Why do you suppose the author began the story this way?
- Who tells the story? Why do you think the author chose this point of view?
- Can you think of a reason for ending the chapter here? What do you expect will happen next? What clues does the author give you?
- How does the author organize the book/story? Do you think this structure works well?
- Can you find an example of foreshadowing?

Reflection

- Explain the title of the book. Can you think of another title?
- What were your thoughts and feelings at the end of the story?
- Why do you think the author chose this ending?
- What might the author have wanted us to learn?
- If you could meet the author, what questions would you ask?
- Using the information you've learned about the author's life, find parts of the story that may have been influenced by the author's own experiences.
- What important symbols did the author include in the story? What do you think they represent?
- Would this book make a good movie? Why or why not? What parts would you leave out? What problems might a director encounter trying to translate the writer's words onto the movie screen?

Putting Questions to Work

Whether you use general author awareness questions or more text-specific questions, what matters most is how you design and use them. When constructing comprehension questions, first ask yourself: Why do I want to ask this? What kind of thinking do I want my students to engage in? Then decide the best format for the questions.

1. Make a large poster listing a few key questions to display in the classroom as a reference point.
2. After reading a short story, divide the class into small groups. Each group is responsible for discussing one question.
3. Use the questions as a springboard for journal writing.
4. Use the questions to stimulate discussion.
5. When assigning a book chapter for homework, give students one question on which to focus.
6. Give students a list of 10 questions to focus on throughout the book. As a book project, have them hand in the written answers. This is especially effective when students are reading different novels. (*Hint*: Make sure to review the questions before students begin.) Monitor progress to ensure students are on the right track.

Not only did these questions lead to more critical thinking and a better author/reader connection but, after using them with several classes, I discovered four distinct advantages.

ADVANTAGES OF AUTHOR AWARENESS QUESTIONS

1. *Students Are More Inclined to Move Ahead and Enjoy the Book.* My students, who were not avid readers to begin with, seemed relieved that they had to concentrate only on 10 to 15 questions for an entire book. Requiring students to answer 10 questions after each chapter breaks the flow and makes reading a chore.

2. *The Teacher Is Relieved of Paperwork Overload.* Ten questions for each chapter makes 100 answers. Multiply this by 20 students, and you get 2,000. Three classes makes 6,000 answers to read and correct. This is unnecessary! Using a generic question list is not laziness. These questions require a great deal of thought, reflection, and writing. Students are learning while you are assessing their comprehension.

3. *There Are No Right or Wrong Answers.* Rather than right or wrong, you are looking for answers that are thoughtful, knowledgeable, well supported, and clearly stated. One problem I always had with chapter questions is what to do when a student gets an answer wrong. For example, if the question is: How much time has passed in Chapter Three? and the student answers incorrectly, do you then write the correct answer on his or her paper? If so, the student hasn't gained much. Should you tell him or her to find the correct answer? Maybe. But by the time you have handed back the questions sheet, the student has already moved on to the next assignment. He or she is likely to simply ask a friend for the answer since it is merely a number. The real problem is not solved: Why didn't the reader know how much time passed in the chapter? Did he or she miss clues from the author? Probably.

Suppose you asked: How does the author let you know how much time has passed in Chapter Three? This question gives the student a focus. He or she is reminded to pay attention to the devices used by the author to indicate time passage. Finally, when you read the student's answer, you can determine if he or she is aware of this. The question can be used for any novel, even when you do not know the answer beforehand because the student must offer proof.

4. *The Questions Work Well with Heterogeneous Groups.* The movement toward mainstreaming and inclusion is strong. Many students arrive in classrooms speaking English as a second language. Whether you are a reading specialist or language arts teacher, you are more than likely to be teaching children with a wide range of reading ability. The beauty of the author awareness questions is that two very different answers can still be valid. Each student goes through a similar process of finding the answer, but the interpretation and depth of response will vary according to ability and reading experience. For example, consider this question: What important symbols did the author include in the story? What do you think they represent?

Student A might answer:

S. E. Hinton uses the sunset as a symbol. It occurs a few times in the story. Even though Ponyboy and Cherry are from different backgrounds, they still share the same sunset. This shows that people can be different but still have some things in common.

Student B might answer:

In the book, The Outsiders, *the author uses the sunset and the color gold as symbols. Ponyboy and Cherry are from different sides of the tracks, yet when they view the sunset together, they are reminded of their common humanity. The beautiful sunset shines for both neighborhoods, rich and poor. The golden color in the sun represents goodness and innocence. That is why Johnny says to Ponyboy, "Stay gold." Ponyboy still has the potential to make his life good.*

Student-Generated Questions

Research supports the idea that training children to formulate effective questions fascilitates their ability to answer comprehension questions. (Manzo, 1969; Raphael, 1982; Risko & Feldman, 1984). Try this experiment. After reading a book chapter or short story as a class, ask the students to assume the role of the teacher. Have them write 10 questions they would ask to check a student's understanding of the story. I have found this to be a better assessment of comprehension than simply giving students a quiz on the story. First of all, in order to generate specific questions, the student must have read the text. Second, an analysis of the questions generated can tell you a great deal about what the student views as important. For example, are most of the questions concerned with recalling specific details? Do the questions call for one-word or one-sentence answers? Do any of the questions require inferential thinking or ask for the reader's insight? Are there a variety of question types? Do any of the questions address the author's voice? Another reason to encourage student-generated questions is that the process of formulating questions requires a reader to think about what he or she has read, to determine what is important, and to practice phrasing a coherent question.

Students like preparing and answering their own questions. It gives them a sense of control and independence. They also tend to think the task is easier than answering a teacher's questions. I have had students design their own chapter tests and exchange them with classmates. This exercise demonstrates the importance of writing clear questions because confusion often arises and the test taker must then seek out the test designer for clarification.

One problem with student-generated questions is that if students answer their own questions, they may not move beyond the recall stage. Students who have difficulty generating higher-level questions will often have difficulty answering them.

Therefore I recommend the modeling and teaching of higher level questioning. The use of author awareness questions is a good starting point.

Techniques for Question Training

Categorizing   Begin by giving students names for different types of questions—for example: Predictions (What will happen next?), Interpretations (Why did this happen?), Recall (How much time has passed?), Detail (What city did they visit?), and Summarization (What happened at the party?).

Title Focus   Before reading a novel or short story, ask students to think of several questions related to the title (Singer, 1978). This is a great focusing exercise as well. Then, after reading a paragraph of the text, ask students what questions pop in their minds.

Group Questioning   Divide students into groups. Have them question each other after reading a story or chapter. I have made a poster of question leads to display in the classroom. This serves as a reference point for group discussion as well as writing questions.

> Why do you suppose…
> How does the author…
> Give an example of…
> Describe…
> Show how…
> When did you first notice…

The 5Ws   Learning the 5Ws—Who, What, Where, When, Why (and hoW)—is particularly useful for students who have difficulty in question formation. This simple technique is crucial for study skills and summary writing.

Let's Fix It   Sometimes, just seeing examples of poorly worded questions can help students learn to generate clear questions. Give written examples of ambiguous questions (such as: What does Tony like best?) and have the students identify the ambiguity. Ask how they would reword each question. Do the same for questions requiring a yes or no answer. Have students restate the question so more elaboration is needed. Then take these questions and have students categorize them by factual or interpretive types.

Look and Ask   Display an unusual or interesting photograph. Ask the children, "What do you want to know about this picture?" List all their questions on the board. Students can evaluate or categorize the questions and speculate on the answers.

Question Me an Answer   Another fun and challenging method of question training is to supply students with an answer to which they must formulate the question. For instance:

> A: *A Wind in the Door.*
> Q: What is the sequel to Madeleine L'Engle's book *A Wrinkle in Time?*

Effective Questions for Critical Reading

Learning to read fiction with a sense of writer can extend to nonfictionl. In addition to good literature, middle school students need practice in comprehending various styles of nonfiction. Essays, editorials, profiles, interviews, columns, personal experiences, and book and movie reviews can be used to develop critical reading. Using magazine and newspaper articles in the reading class captures student interest and stimulates discussion. This type of reading puts students in touch with their world and builds general knowledge. It can improve ability to read content material in social studies and science class as well.

Questioning Strategies for Nonfiction

Keep in mind that effective comprehension questions assess and instruct at the same time. This will help you move beyond just asking students about main idea and details. Push your students to read between the lines, identify an author's purpose and organization, detect biases, and evaluate the accuracy and quality of the text.

When using nonfiction in a reading lesson, begin by having students survey the source, author, and title of the article, then generate predictions about its content. Next, provide introductory information and ask students what they already know about the topic and what they might like to find out. Introduce key vocabulary words, and then give students a purpose for reading.

Next, have students read silently or aloud, depending on the length and difficulty of the article. If needed (or for variety), read the article to the class. You may want them to stop midpoint to evaluate comprehension. What have they learned so far? What didn't they understand?

An informal discussion can follow after reading. Try to let the students do most of the talking. Afterwards, use author awareness questions to encourage critical thinking. Depending on the topic and form of the article, you may want to try other extension activities.

This approach facilitates active reading. The students' background knowledge is connected to their reading. The reader learns to identify attitudes, ideas, and opinions of an author rather than viewing the nonfiction text as voiceless and encyclopedic.

AUTHOR AWARENESS QUESTIONS FOR NONFICTION

1. Who wrote this? What audience do you think the author had in mind? Why?
2. What was the author's purpose? How do you know?
3. What category of nonfiction is this? How has the author organized the information? Does this work?
4. Can you find examples of humor, propaganda, anecdotes, sensory words, sarcasm, or emotional appeal? Why did the author use these techniques?
5. What questions came to mind during and after reading? Was the author's meaning clear to you? If not, why?
6. Does the author express his or her own opinions or biases? Support your answer with examples.
7. Write five questions that can be answered from reading the article and five that require further information.

Putting the Questions to Work

These questions are difficult to answer; in fact, most middle school students lack experience with this type of questioning and thinking. Initially, introduce just one or two questions after each reading. Students need to learn *how* to think about the questions. For example, to answer question 2, students will need to learn the various purposes of writing (persuasion, entertainment, instruction, etc.). Question 4 requires understanding the meaning of terms such as *propaganda* and *anecdote* and practice in detecting these writing techniques.

In the beginning, you will need to discuss the questions and answers with the entire class. After students understand the *meaning* of the questions and have had direct instruction in using them, they can work with a partner and write down their responses. This preview work is essential and too often overlooked. Eventually, students should have experience selecting nonfiction pieces to read and answering the questions on their own.

Developing a Schema for Nonfiction

As students read a variety of nonfiction and analyze structure and content, they build a schema (mental construction) for specific genres. This aids comprehension because students are able to make predictions and recognize an author's purpose. Question 6 helps students focus on the specific characteristics and structure of different nonfiction genres. For example, after reading three columns from a popular *Boston Globe* columnist, my students discovered that the columns were written in the first person, personal opinions were expressed, anecdotes were used, and the writing appealed to the readers' emotions. The students also discovered that a column could be humorous or serious. We then read a column by a different author and compared its form and content to the first columnist.

After reading articles on health and science topics, my students discovered the use of subheadings, charts, and side bars and how these features can alert them to the main ideas of the text

Textbook Troubles

This type of reading activity provides an excellent preparation for textbook study. Over the years that I have worked privately with students on developing study skills, I have always been struck by the absence of voice in science and social studies textbooks. The dull, lifeless writing not only bores students but it also makes reading all the more difficult. Perhaps the new interactive technology will make textbooks obsolete, but until then, I think that reading specialists, resource room teachers, and content teachers as well, should help students learn to read textbooks. Reading consultants could assist content teachers by giving them specific strategies for making textbooks more readable.

One example is to have students peruse the textbook at the beginning of the year before any reading assignments are given. Ask students where they think the information in the textbook came from. Have them read the author credits, consultant list, and acknowledgments. Discuss how textbooks get written and the issue of censorship and neutrality. Then have the children examine the table of contents. How does it seemed to be organized? Which topics interest them?

Finally, students should flip through the book. How many pages are there? Are there lots of pictures? Tables? Charts? How are the chapters structured? Don't forget the index—make sure students know when and how to use it.

Sometimes, just admitting that a text is on the dull side makes kids feel at ease. However, it is important to point out that there are techniques to textbook reading and that learning the tricks will aid their study in high school and college.

Poor readers, in particular, have difficulty comprehending textbooks because they are unable to see the key ideas or to select significant information. One way to overcome this is to teach students to recognize an author's organizational pattern (McNeil, 1984). The predominant organizational structures in textbooks are:

Cause and effect
Listing/enumerating
Comparison and contrast
Problem and solution
Time order

Students first need practice in identifying the patterns. Begin with short selections and teach signal words that aid pattern recognition.

CAUSE/EFFECT	COMPARISON/ CONTRAST	TIME/ORDER
Consequently	Similarly	Later
As a result	On the other hand	Presently
Finally	Whereas	Afterward
Thus	In contrast	Soon
Therefore	Unlike	Next

You can create your pattern guides. Figure 2–1 show two simple pattern guides that alert students to the author's organizational pattern. As students use each guide, they also gain practice in skimming, note taking, and locating key ideas.

Results

Although using this method of critical reading takes time and direct instruction, I enthusiastically recommend it for challenging students' thinking and for developing active readers. Most important, this kind of reading asks students (and teaches them *how*) to analyze information. This is an ability that research and standardized test scores indicate our students are lacking.

FIGURE 2–1   Sample Pattern Guides

Chapter 7: Types of Government

Comparison/Contrast

One way authors help you understand information and ideas is by comparing and contrasting. *Comparing* means showing how two ideas are *alike*. *Contrasting* means showing how they are *different*. On pages 55–60, the author compares and contrasts two forms af government, capitalism and socialism. Fill in the following chart as you read.

DIFFERENCES

Capitalism	*Socialism*
1.	1.
2.	2.
3.	3.
4.	4.

*   *   *

Chapter 5: The Brain Hemispheres

Lists

Authors often list important names or key ideas. On page 120 of your textbook, the author has listed the division of the cerebral (brain) hemispheres (areas). Write the names of each hemisphere and its function.

Areas of the Brain Hemisphere

1. _____   Function a. _____ b. _____
2. _____   Function a. _____ b. _____
3. _____   Function a. _____ b. _____

Genre Study

Learning to recognize the characteristics of a genre—such as fables, tall tales, folktales, science fiction, mystery, myths, and contemporary fiction—develops a student's sense of story and enables him or her to make better predictions while reading. In addition to aiding comprehension, understanding story structure gives the student a framework for writing.

Dorothy Strickland (1987) of Teachers College in New York suggests that teachers first immerse students in a genre through shared reading, discussion, dramatizing, and retelling of stories. For example, in studying folktales, students might listen to recorded tales, compare those of different cultures, discuss settings, and act out scenes. This helps students internalize the features of the genre.

The next step is have the youngsters identify these special features. Strickland suggests that teachers ask students to create charts based on what they have learned about a specific genre such as a mystery. I have had students create genre "recipes." Here is one for fairy tales.

FAIRY TALE RECIPE

Prepare a setting of long ago.
Shape into a forest, village, castle,
or imaginary kingdom or faraway land.
Add imaginary characters—try kings,
queens, fairies, witches, maidens,
woodcutters, and beasts.
Sprinkle with magic and the number 3.
Divide the batter into good and evil.
Mix in a problem to solve.
Garnish with wishes, spells, and deception.
Bake for many years until the ending
looks golden.

Another valuable activity is for students to compare different versions of fairy tales. One could begin with the original "Cinderella" in *Grimms' Tales for Young and Old: The Complete Stories* translated by Ralph Manhein (Doubleday, 1977) and compare it to the numerous other retellings such as the one told by the Algonquin Indians in *World Tales*. This is a wonderful way to demonstrate an author's interpretation and style. Students can compare use of language, opening paragraphs, endings, and character development as well as illustrations.

After this engaging introduction, students should then be ready to write their own fairy tales, mysteries, legends, and so on. For younger or less abled students, an intermediary step would be for the teacher and students to create the story together. Lists of variants of the same story to explore for genre study may be found at the end of this chapter. (An extended teaching idea also may be found at the end of the chapter.)

Genre Comparison

Genre	Characters	Setting	Plot	Example
Science fiction				
Fairy tales				
Myths				
Fables				
Folktales				
Historical fiction				
Fantasy				

Genre Comparison

Genre	Characters	Setting	Plot	Example
Mystery				
Adventure				
Survival				
Memoir				
Contemporary				
Horror				

Literary Terms Project

Put together a book of literary terms. Each page should address the meaning of one term. Show that you understand the definition by giving examples and using illustrations, pictures, or diagrams. Be creative and colorful.

Literary Terms

1. Plot
2. Characterization
3. Setting
4. Mood
5. Theme
6. Imagery
7. Protagonist
8. Antagonist
9. Simile
10. Metaphor
11. Symbolism
12. Dialogue
13. Genre
14. Tension
15. Conflict
16. Climax
17. Point-of-view
18. Style

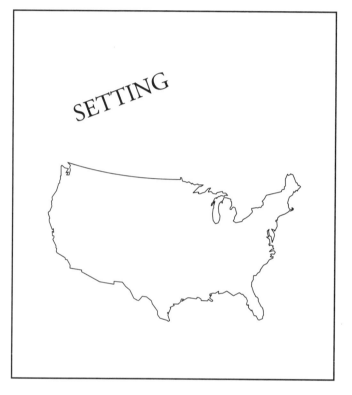

Tolkien's Beginning

After completing the Tolkien beginning worksheet, read aloud from the second paragraph of *The Hobbit*, which describes, in detail, the underground home.

Ask the children, "Was your prediction correct?"

Continue with, "Mr. Tolkien doesn't yet tell us much more about the hobbit. What can you infer about the hobbit's character from its home?"

Next, ask, "Why do you think Mr. Tolkien included so many details about the hobbit's hole?"

Then "Let's listen to the description again. Which words does the author use to give you a mind picture?"

A good activity to accompany this teaching idea is to have the students draw mental pictures of the hobbit's hole.

A Solitary Blue

After completing the Voight beginning worksheet, supplement with the following ideas:

1. After dicussing Cynthia Voight's opening to *Solitary Blue*, have the students write their own openings that involve a letter or note. Do this yourself.
2. Write your opening on the board or overhead projector. Ask the students to generate questions.
3. Next, ask the children to help create a possible story line. Allow for brainstorming.
4. Divide the students into groups to share their openings.
5. For extra credit, challenge the students over the next week to find another book that opens with a letter or note.
6. Make a display of Cynthia Voight's books.
   Homecoming   *Jackaroo*
   Dicey's Song   *Izzy, Willy-Nilly*
   The Callender Papers   *Stories about Rosie*
   Building Blocks   *Come a Stranger*
   The Runner

Growing a Poem

When composing poems, student writers often start with broad topics such as summer, friendship, and love. The resulting poem is often too general and lacks impact. You can help students develop the essence of a poem by "opening" their senses, and encouraging them to notice the details of their surroundings.

1. Give students a copy of a few poems that demonstrate a detail. A simple one is "Icicles" by Barbara Juster Esbensen in *April Bubbles Chocolate: An ABC of Poetry*, selected by Lee Bennett Hopkins (Simon & Schuster, 1994). Discuss how the poet developed a poem around a specific object, idea, or event.

2. Try a class poem. On the board, draw a large tree with branches. Then select a focal point in the classroom, such as a door or a window. Write the name of this focal point inside the tree trunk. Have students brainstorm word association with the object. Help them along by asking: What does it feel like? What does it look like? What does it make you think about? What is it used for? What unusual things might happen to it? Write responses on the tree's branches. Finally, synthesize the associations into a poem with help from the class. Write the results on the board or overhead projector.

3. Now pick a different focal point in the room and have students do the same exercise on their own. Set a time limit if necessary. Try this yourself. Encourage students to share their poems with the class. (Or you can collect the poems and read them anonymously.) You and your students will be amazed at the number of different ways there are to think about a simple desk!

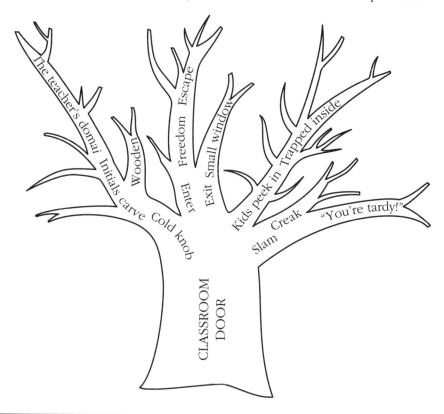

Recognizing Style

Have several students take turns writing their signatures on the board. Let the students point out the differences and similarities among the signatures.

Say to the students, "Just like each person has a particular signature, each writer has a particular style. If I asked each of you to write a story about a dog, I would have [number of students] different stories. Two painters painting the same mountain will not produce the exact same painting. Style makes the difference."

1. Tell the students to compare texts that have the same content and structure but that vary in language. For example, rewrite a local news article in a more poetic or emotional style. Have students read both articles and note the differences.
2. Children's picture books are particularly helpful for teaching students about style. Gather several books by Dr. Seuss, Eric Carle, Ezra Jack Keats, and Bill Peet. Divide the children into study groups. Have them focus on book format, language, point of view, plot/topic, characters, and illustrations. Allow each group to present their stylistic findings to the class.
3. Read aloud the first page of a novel by an author with a distinct style (such as Paul Zindel, Judy Blume, and Paula Danziger). Ask the students to describe these authors' "signatures." Record their observations on the board.
4. Encourage students to try out elements of an author's style in their own writing. For example, after reading *The Pigman* or *A Begonia for Miss Applebaum* by Paul Zindel, students might try writing a story in the first person from two view points. Let students try composing a poem in the style of their favorite poet such as Emily Dickinson, Shel Silverstein, or e. e. cummings.

References

Farr, Roger. (1989). Speech given at the Annual Conference of the International Reading Association, New Orleans.

Holt, Suzzane J., & Vacca, Jo Anne L. (1984). *Composing and Comprehending.* Urbana, IL: National Conference on Research in English. ERIC Clearinghouse on Reading and Communications Skills, pp. 175–180.

Krieger, Evelyn. (1990). Developing reading comprehension through author awareness. *The Journal of Reading, 33,* 618–619.

Krieger, Evelyn. (1990, October). Effective questioning for critical reading. *Reading Today.*

Krieger, Evelyn. (1991, February). Effective questioning for critical reading of nonfiction. *Reading Today.*

Manzo, A. V. (1969). The ReQuest procedure. *Journal of Reading, 13,* 123–126.

McNeil, John D. (1984). *Reading Comprehension: New Directions for Classroom Practice.* GLenview, IL: Scott, Foresman, pp. 30–31.

Pennac, Daniel. (1994). *Better Than Life*. Toronto: Coach House, Press, p. 153.

Raphael, T. E. (1982). Teaching children question-answering strategies. *The Reading Teacher, 36*, 186–191.

Risko, V. J., & Feldman, N. (1984). Teaching young remedial readers to generate questions as they read. *Reading Psychology, 23*, 54–64.

Shanahan, Timonthy. (1988). The reading-writing relationship: Seven principles for instruction. *Reading Teacher, 41*, 636–647.

Singer, Harry. (1978). Active comprehension. *Reading Teacher, 31*, 901–908.

Strickland, Dorothy. (1987). Literature: Key element in the language and reading program. In Bernice Cullinan (Ed.), *Children's Literature in the Reading Program* (pp. 71–74). Newark, DE: International Reading Association.

Voight, Cynthia. (1990). In Donald Gallo (Ed.), *Speaking for Ourselves* (p. 217). National Council for Teachers of English.

Children's Fiction

Avi. (1990). *The True Confessions of Charlotte Doyle*. New York: Avon.

Duder, Tessa. (1989). *In Lane Three, Alex Archer*. Boston: Houghton Mifflin.

Hamilton, Virginia. (1993). *Sweet Whispers, Brother Rush*. New York: Avon.

Hassler, Jon. (1977). *Four Miles to Pinecone*. New York: Warne.

Spinelli, Jerry. (1992). *Maniac Magee*. New York: Harper.

Tolkien, J. R. R. (1966). *The Hobbitt*. Boston: Houghton Mifflin.

Uchida, Yoshiki. (1978). *Journey Home*. New York: Atheneum.

Voight, Cynthia. (1993). *A Solitary Blue*. New York: Scholastic.

Zindel, Paul. (1968). *The Pigman*. New York: Harper Collins.

Zindel, Paul. (1989). *A Begonia for Miss Applebaum*. New York: Harper and Row.

Zindel, Paul. (1991). *The Pigman & Me*. New York: Harper Collins.

Poetry Anthologies

Knudson, R. R., & Swenson, May (Eds.). *American Sports Poems*. New York: Orchard, 1988.

Morrison, Lillian. (1985). *The Break Dance Kids: Poems of Sport, Motion, and Locomotion*. New York: Lothrop, Lee & Shepard.

Peck, Richard. (Ed.). (1990). *Sounds and Silences: Poetry for Now*. New York: Dell.

Silverstein, Shel. (1974). *Where the Sidewalk Ends*. New York: Harper and Row.

Soto, Gary. (1985). *Black Hair*. Pittsburgh: University of Pittsburgh Press.

Viorst, Judith. (1981). *If I Were In Charge of the World and Other Worries*. New York: Aladin.

Poetry Resources

Fergusson, Rosaline. (1985). *The Penguin Rhyming Dictionary*. New York: Viking.

Hopkins, Lee Bennett. (1987). *Pass the Poetry, Please?* (rev. ed.). New York: Harper and Row.

Jeneczko, Paul B. (Ed.). (1983). *Poet Speak: In Their Work, About Their Work*. Scardale, NY: Bradbury.

Koch, Kenneth. (1970). *Wishes, Lies, and Dreams: Teaching Children to Write Poetry*. New York: Chelsea House.

Sears, Peter (Ed.). (1990). *Gonna Bake Me A Rainbow Poem: A Student Guide to Writing Poetry.* New York: Scholastic.

Waley, Arthur. (1919, 1947). *Translations from the Chinese.* New York: Knopf.

Aesop's Tales

Aesop's Fables. (1980). Retold by Arnold Lobel. New York: Harper and Row.

The Fables of Aesop: 143 Moral Tales Retold. (1976). Selected and edited by Ruth Spriggs. Illustrated by Frank Barber.

Folk/Fairy Tales

Beauty. (1978). Robert McKinley. New York: Harper.

Beauty and the Beast. (1989). Retold by Jan Brett. New York: *Clarion.*

Favorite Folktales from Around the World. (1986). Edited by Jane Yolen. New York: Pantheon.

A Taste for Quiet and Other Disquieting Tales. (1982). Judith Gorog. New York: Philomel.

Twelve Tales by Hans Christian Andersen. (1994). Translated and illustrated by Erik Blegvad. New York: McElderry/Macmillan.

World Tales. (1979). Collected by Idries Shah. New York: Harcourt.

Myths

The Olympians: Great Gods and Goddesses of Ancient Greece. (1984). New York: Holiday House.

Russell, William. (1988). *Classic Myths to Read Aloud.* New York: Crown.

Hawthorne, Nathaniel. (1994). *A Wonder Book for Girls and Boys.* New York: Knopf.

3

Writing as Readers

I cannot read a book anymore without wondering how the author achieved an effect that I like. But my pleasure in reading hasn't diminished. To the contrary, I find extra delight when the techniques below the surface reveal themselves, perhaps only after several readings. The techniques have a beauty of their own. And I can steal them, posthaste, for my own writing.

—Alan Lightman (1994)

The Reading/Writing Connection

During my quest to help students move from passive reading to active reading through author awareness, wonderful things began to happen. First, I saw student interest piqued as they learned about the real voice behind the printed page. My students were delighted to encounter these new voices outside the classroom.

> "Guess what, Ms. Krieger? Maya Angelou was on a talk show yesterday."
> "Hey, did you guys see that Halloween special? It was all about Edgar Allan Poe's 'The Raven.'"
> "My parents took me to Louisa Alcott's house."

Learning about the lives of authors led my students to seek out their books in the library—no more randomly choosing a book by its cover (or thickness!). Not only were my students reading more but they were also thinking about what they had read.

The author awareness activities I used for comprehension helped students develop vocabulary for talking about a written work. "Ray Bradbury uses awesome metaphors," Meredith, an eighth-grader, told me. I had to agree. It was a pleasure to see students moving beyond simple statements such as "It was an exciting book" or "The author uses good description." For example, when a student didn't like a book, he or she could now state *why:* "There wasn't enough dialogue" or "I didn't come to care about the characters."

At the same time my students were developing their reading ability, their writing ability dramatically improved. This happened *without* a separate writing curriculum. The author awareness reading activities taught students to look for a writer's special effects such as humor, imagery, flashbacks, suspense, and characterization. In learning what makes a piece of writing effective, my students began to experiment using these techniques in their own writing. The result was more vivid and engaging stories and compositions. Voices emerged. Reading with a sense of writer helped them to write with a sense of reader.

The studies of researchers and teachers Donald Graves and Jane Hansen (1983) support this reading/writing connection. Graves and Hansen found that even children as young as age 6 or 7 could develop a more sophisticated concept of author that improved both reading and writing ability. During a year-long writing program conducted in Ellen Blackburn's first-grade classroom in Somersworth, New Hampshire, the children wrote and drew every day, published stories, and shared them with classmates.

The sharing activities centered around the prestigious "Author's Chair," where student-authors read their work and teachers read trade books aloud. The children asked the child-author questions about the work. When a teacher read from a professional trade book, he or she always gave the author's background and encouraged the children to comment or question.

The children's stories were published in a hard cover and kept in the classroom library alongside the conventional books. The student books served as the main texts for reading instruction. The children read their books to each other and offered feedback. This served to reinforce the idea of writing with a sense of audience. As the children read and wrote daily, the two processes became integrated.

Shouldn't this be our goal for older children as well? Why are our middle school students so often stuck in the mechanical stage of writing? Is it that teachers have focused on this first, if not alone? Unfortunately, the red pen still lives in many classrooms today. When compositions come back full of corrections at the mechanical level, a student sees this as primary importance. Also, since right and wrong are more clearly defined in grammar and punctuation, rather than in composing, children fixate on the former.

Try a simple experiment in your classroom. (This is most effective at the beginning of the year.) Make copies of a short essay that contains mechanical errors but is also in need of revision in form, content, and style. Ask students to assume the role of teacher. Have each student write suggestions to the author for revising the essay. Do not offer assistance. Collect the papers and study them carefully. Can students recognize problems with clarity? Can they offer effective feedback? Can they identify grammatical errors? And if so, do they concentrate on this alone?

This exercise will quickly tell you how much your students know about the writing process. In fact, it is also a good predictor of writing *ability*. (Try this again at the end of the year or term to assess growth.)

Although we certainly want our students to use correct grammar and spelling, this skill alone does not produce interesting, lively, or persuasive writing. You may be surprised to find that the student who can recognize deficiencies at the content level, *even while missing mechanical errors,* is often a better writer than the student who is proficient only in grammar and punctuation. My own classroom research supports this conclusion.

I also found that poor readers were more likely to focus purely on mechanics. When asked to critique a composition, these students had trouble seeing beyond punctuation, spelling, and grammar errors. I see two possible explanations for this. First, remedial readers tend to receive most of their instruction at the mechanical and literal levels. Second, since they have less literary experience, poor readers have not yet built a schema to recognize and talk about what makes good writing. Poor readers are almost always poor writers.

In a study conducted by Graves and Hansen (1983), the researchers found that students were stuck in the "sounding out" phase, but eventually were able to develop a more differentiated concept of author by actively composing in both reading and writing. The researchers identified three developmental phases that led to a more sophisticated sense of authorship. Moving through these phases, the students learned about topic selection, adding information, text organization, and rewriting. In the third phase, the children demonstrated a high level of author awareness. The child rewrites with a sense that the

> *class will ask when he reads the piece from the author's chair.... In both reading and writing, the children have a sense of process and are especially free of the "sounding out" component so dominant in earlier statements. Such freedom lifts the children into more thinking about information and the content and organization of what authors actually do in writing. (p. 180)*

Graves and Hansen concluded:

> *Children who learn to exercise options [in writing] become more assertive in dealing with other authors. At first an author is distant, then an author is self, finally the self-author questions all authors and assertive readers emerge. (p. 181)*

Activities such as journal writing, Author's Chair, student publishing, shared stories, and writer's workshops can be used in upper elementary and junior high school. Such activities are enjoyable, motivating, and encourage active learning. Reading and writing become integrated and both abilities are enhanced.

The decline in U.S. students' writing skills has received national attention. It is common sense that poor readers are unlikely to be terrific writers. We can facilitate writing ability by integrating reading and writing instruction. We must also move beyond the teaching of comprehension at the literal level. We must move beyond simply testing whether students understand a story. We must help children of all ages and abilities to hear the author's voice at the same time they are finding their own.

An Author's Special Effects

I find the analogy of "special effects" particularly helpful and appealing to youngsters. Labeling these *special effects* helps students recognize and incorporate them in their reading and writing. After introducing students to these special effects, you might focus on activities that emphasize an author's particular strength. For example, try organizing a display of library books in the following manner: Perfect Plots, Colorful Characters, Delightfully Descriptive, and Page Turners. This helps students select books from a different perspective and develops their literary tastes.

Just as a student artist studies the masters, the students in your classroom need models of great writing in order to become effective writers. Over the years, I have collected illustrative passages from a variety of literature. If I am teaching a lesson on effective use of metaphors and similes, for example, I might pull out Ray Bradbury's short story, "All Summer in a Day." When a student is struggling with creating crisp dialogue, I can hand him or her excerpts from Richard Peck's fast-paced thrillers.

Begin training your eyes and ears to spot examples of effective writing in novels, short stories, essays, poems, and articles. Mark pages, underline paragraphs, clip articles, and copy book passages. Soon, you will have your own special effects collection to inspire and instruct budding young writers. I am pleased to share some of my finds with you at the end of this chapter.

Here is a cure for the midyear doldrums (a particularly bad condition in cold climates!). Choose a suspenseful novel to read as a class, preferably a mystery to be solved. I have had success with Agatha Christie's *Ten Little Indians* (also titled *And Then There Were None).*

I begin by presenting Agatha's Christie's life, which is fascinating and brimming with mystery. Students also study a map of England, with particular attention to the Devonshire area, where the story is set and Christie grew up. I then preview the book's publishing history and story setting.

The book is heavy on dialogue with difficult vocabulary, so I review key words before reading each chapter in class. Students read along with an audio recording, which brings each character's voice to life. Since the details of their lives and personalities are paramount, I have students record the gathered information on a chart. For reinforcement, students create a character bulletin board, play "Who Am I?" and match quotes to characters.

Once students are hooked on the plot, I move more quickly. At this point, their hypotheses start forming and students enjoy debating and speculating. As the plot thickens, students often beg me to reveal the answer (which is not simple!). Agatha Christie leaves us hanging at the end of each chapter. This drives the children crazy. One year, three boys gathered after school to read ahead a few chapters! This was especially a treat for me, considering how long I had tried to *push* these boys to read.

Although a challenging book, particularly for remedial readers, *Ten Little Indians* contains so many surprises, twists, and quirks that your students will push themselves to read carefully and closely—and to think! This is just what you need to spice up your class during the midyear doldrums.

Getting Started

The following exercises will help your students learn to write with a sense of reader. The reproducible activity sheets can be used as an extension of larger lessons, homework assignments, or group tasks. (Extended teaching ideas may be found at the end of the chapter.) In ordering the skills and concepts, I have intentionally built on the previous lessons, moving from part to whole. If you are working under the demands of a skills-based curriculum, this section should be particularly helpful.

It's All in the Details

How would you describe a house? A tree? Or a car?

Knowing a variety of words to describe objects will help you paint a picture for the reader. Let's begin with feature words. Complete the list below. Aim for interesting descriptive words, not overly used words such as *big* and *little*. Keep this list for future reference.

SIZE WORDS

_____
_____
_____
_____
_____
_____

TEXTURE WORDS

_____
_____
_____
_____
_____
_____

SHAPE WORDS

_____
_____
_____
_____
_____
_____

COLOR WORDS

Red   _____
_____

Green _____
_____

White _____
_____

Black _____
_____

Blue   _____
_____
_____

Use Your Senses

We learn about the world through our five senses: sight, smell, hearing, taste, and touch. Good writers use *sensory* words to help the reader experience the story. Watch how the use of sensory words can breathe life into the following sentence. Which sense is evoked in each sentence?

It was a windy spring day.

The wind whistled. _____

There was a scent of damp leaves. _____

The warm wind lifted his kite. _____

The bare trees swayed in slow motion. _____

As the rain began to fall, she caught the first drops on her tongue.
_____

Your Turn

You are writing a scene set in a fast-food restaurant. Write descriptive sentences that use the five senses to bring the reader inside.

Sight_____

_____

Sound _____

_____

Smell _____

_____

Taste _____

_____

Touch _____

_____

Authors with Good Senses

John Steinbeck is a master at writing vivid description and using sensory details. In his book *The Long Valley*, Steinbeck describes a valley family living in a tent as they are preparing breakfast.

I was close now and I could smell frying bacon and baking bread, the warmest, pleasantest odors I know. From the east the light grew swiftly. I came near to the stove and stretched my hands out to it and shivered over when the warmth struck me. Then the tent flap jerked up and a young man came out and an older man followed him. They were dressed in new blue dungarees and in new dungaree coats with the brass buttons shining.

Find the sensory words Steinbeck uses.

Smell _____

Touch _____

Sight _____

Consider this sentence: The man's hands grew cold. Can you improve it so that the reader feels *how* cold and in what *way* the cold affected the man's hands? _____

_____

_____

Jack London lived a life of adventure and wrote about it, too. In his famous short story, "To Build a Fire," he describes a man and his dog fighting to survive the cold wilderness. Can you feel the cold in this passage?

All a man had to do was keep his head, and he was all right. Any man who was a man could travel alone. But it was surprising, the rapidity with which his cheeks and nose were freezing. And he had not thought his fingers could go lifeless in so short a time. Lifeless they were, for he could scarcely make them move together to grip a twig, and they seemed remote from his body and from him. When he touched a twig, he had to look and see whether or not he had hold of it. The wires were pretty well down between him and his finger-ends.

What is happening to the man's hands?_____

_____

Sensory Word List

The sense of sight is probably the easist to describe in words. Describing how things *look* is also the most common use of sensory writing. Using the other four senses in writing is not as easy, yet using them can make the difference between ordinary writing and sensational writing.

Brainstorm several sensory words to use when describing things or places. Save for later use. (*Hint:* It may help to think of specific things or settings.)

SOUNDS

_____

_____

_____

_____

_____

_____

TASTES

_____

_____

_____

_____

_____

_____

SMELLS

_____

_____

_____

_____

_____

_____

TOUCH

_____

_____

_____

_____

_____

_____

Show Me!

Writers use *sensory details* to help our minds form pictures of what things look, sound, feel, smell, and taste like.

Your Turn

Expand each sentence to include sensory details so that the reader has a clear mind picture.

Example: The girl looked sad.

Revision: The girl's dark eyes were missing the spark of her youth. They stared into the distance, as if searching for a ray of light.

1. Mr. Singer was a large man. _____

_____

_____

2. The chocolate cream pie was delicious. _____

_____

_____

3. The house on the corner looked haunted. _____

_____

_____

4. It feels nice to walk barefoot on the grass. _____

_____

_____

5. I could hear the train passing by our house each night. _____

_____

_____

6. She could smell the soup cooking. _____

_____

_____

Writing the Right Word

The famous writer Mark Twain once said the difference between the right word and the almost right word is the difference between lightning and a lightning bug. What do you think he meant?

_____

_____

Words are the writer's paintbrush. The right words give color to the pages. For example, suppose a character in a story said, "I bought a new car." What picture comes to your mind? Now suppose the writer of the story revised the sentence like this: "I bought a new Chevy convertible." A completely different picture comes to mind—a *specific* picture. The reader SEES. That is the writer's goal.

Change each general noun to a specific noun.

dog	_____	town	_____
flower	_____	tree	_____
house	_____	reptile	_____
man	_____	money	_____
fruit	_____	clothes	_____
shoes	_____	ball	_____
sound	_____	book	_____
city	_____	building	_____
doctor	_____	candy	_____
bird	_____	newspaper	_____
toy	_____	illness	_____
team	_____	relative	_____

Setting the Scene

The *setting* is more than just where the story happens. A book can have several settings. In creating a setting, the author must consider season, year, weather, country, state, city, as well as the specific place in which events occur, such as a courthouse, battlefield, or schoolbus. Finally, the writer must use details to create a sense of place. The setting then comes to life.

What words and phrases does the author use to create the setting in the story you are reading?

YEAR/DECADE   **SEASON**   **COUNTRY/CITY/TOWN**

PLACE(S) OF MAIN EVENTS

1. _____
   _____

2. _____
   _____

3. _____
   _____

4. _____
   _____

Choose a specific *scene* in the story where one episode or event occurs. What words or phrases does the author use to let the readers "see" and "feel" the place?

Painting a Place

A sense of *place* is an important part of many great stories. Remember the farm and barnyard in *Charlotte's Web? The Land of Oz?* The English manor in *A Secret Garden?* In *The Stone-Faced Boy,* Paula Fox paints the reader a picture of the village where the characters go to school. She uses the four seasons to frame the picture.

> *In the fall, apples rolled down from the orchard and collected in the ditches on either side of the road. In the winter, the snow plow came and exploded the snow into two high banks in which the children sometimes found an old yellow apple frozen into marble. In spring, the ditches filled with lively streams of water that emptied into Currey Pond. In summer, the streams dried up, and black snakes wriggled out from the old stone walls to lie on the road and sun themselves.*

Your Turn

Paint a picture of a place where you live or have lived, using the seasons to show change. (*Hint:* Use details and sensory words to make your picture glow.)

_____

_____

_____

_____

_____

Where in the World Is...?

Can you match the place to the story?

1. Narnia _____

2. Swiss Alps _____

3. Never Never Land _____

4. The English Moor _____

5. Metropolitan Museum Art_____

6. Prydain _____

7. Camelot _____

8. Middle-earth _____

9. Redwall Abbey_____

10. Emerald City _____

*From the Mixed-up Files of
  Mrs. Basil E. Frankweiler*

The Wizard of Oz

*The Lion, the Witch,
  and the Wardrobe*

Heidi

Lassie

The Book of Three

Peter Pan

A Wrinkle in Time

Lord of the Rings

The Secret Garden

Mossflower

The Legends of King Arthur

Vivacious Verbs

Verbs have power. Verbs move your writing along. But not all verbs are alike. Beware of lazy verbs!

Jack hit the ball hard.

Maya ran home quickly.

The man spoke softly.

She walked toward the door quietly.

What's wrong with these verbs? They limp along, that's what! The writer has tried to liven up the verb by using an adverb. Why not hunt for a strong verb instead? Study the difference.

Jack smacked the ball.

Maya raced home.

The man whispered.

She crept toward the door.

Get the idea? The right verb can paint a perfect picture.

Your Turn

Give these lazy verbs a lift.

1. Jason *looked* inside the window of the strange house.

_____

2. The crowd *yelled loudly* as Karen hit a home run.

_____

3. I *slowly sat down* in my chair feeling defeated.

_____

4. Evan *laughed hard* at his brother's antics.

_____

5. The thunder *made* a *loud sound*.

_____

Special Effects

Actions can help paint a picture. A character might sneer, snort, sneeze, or snicker. Each of these actions can show the reader something.

Look around you. Make a list of common actions. Then list what the action may show.

pat on the back   encouragement
a smile   attraction, warmth
handshake   acceptance, winning
blinking one's eyes   nervousness

Adapted from Sandy Asher, *Wild Words! How to Train Them to Tell Stories* (New York: Walker, 1989).

Action! Action!

Writers use powerful verbs to create a feeling of action. Strong verbs give life to the story.

In *The Contender,* Robert Lipsyte is an expert at using strong action verbs. In this scene, 14-year-old Alfred makes a first-time visit to Donatelli's Gym in Harlem where boxers train. Mr. Lipsyte makes us feel as if we are watching the action through Alfred's eyes.

Half-naked bodies were jumping and twisting and jerking around, bells rang, the peanut bag went rackety-rackety-rackety, ropes swish-slapped against the sqeaking floorboards, someone screamed, "TIME," gasping voices, "uh... uh...uh-uh," and an enormous black belly rushed past, spraying sweat like a lawn sprinkler. Alfred shrank back against the door.

Slowly he picked out objects he had seen before. The heavy bag was swinging wildly on its chain as the boy with the enormous belly battered it with fists as big as cantaloupes. The peanut bag was rattling against the round board as a skinny white boy with hunched shoulders beat it into a brown blur. Near the medical scale, two Puerto Ricans were jabbing at their reflections in full-length mirrors. They were quick as cats. Other boys were jumping rope, jerking up and down like mechanical jacks-in-the box, or straining on leather floor mats until their neck cords popped, or slamming medicine balls into each other's stomachs. In the ring, their heads encased by black leather guards, two fighters danced around each other, ducking, bobbing, bouncing on and off the quivering ropes. A stick-thin old black man with white hair was yelling at them, "Faster, faster, pick it up."

1. Underline each action verb.

2. Follow Mr. Lipsyte's example. Find stronger verbs to replace these weaker verbs. For example: Brent *walked* into the room could be changed to: Brent *tip-toed* into the room.

    a. Ellen *sat* in the chair.   _____

    b. The boy *ran* home.   _____

    c. The baby *cried.*   _____

    d. Shira *hit* the ball.   _____

    e. They *went* to the circus.   _____

    f. "I'm leaving!" she *said.*   _____

Colorful Characters

Lucy is a student about your age who wants to introduce a character in a story she is writing. Here is a physical description in Lucy's first draft.

Ten-year-old Delilia had brown hair and wore glasses. She was tall and grace-ful and liked to wear dresses. She spoke quietly since she felt shy around people.

Does Lucy's description of Delilia really help you *see* her? Although Lucy has a good start, she could do a lot more to bring Delilia to life. What are your suggestions?

_____

_____

Lucy asked her father to critique the description. Here is what he said: "Have you ever noticed how many shades of *brown* hair there are? Perhaps you could make Delilia seem more real by using interesting details. What kind of glasses did she wear? Did she wear them all the time? Was she taller than everyone in her class? What kind of dresses did Delilia prefer? What did her quiet voice sound like?"

Revising

Here is Lucy's second try. Compare this to her first description of Delilia.

Ten-year-old Delilia had hair the color of chestnuts. She always wore it in two perfect long braids. Her classmates had never seen her without her wire glasses. Delilia preferred wearing pale, frilly dresses to school. She carried her tall, thin body quite gracefully. Her voice was more like a whisper since she was shy around people.

When Lucy showed her classmate Maria this draft, she replied: "I can really see Delilia and I'm interested in knowing more."

Change the *general* description to a specific description.

1. blonde hair   hair like sunshine
2. long hair   _____
3. small eyes   _____

4. small nose _____

5. fancy dress _____

6. white shirt _____

Use your imagination to finish these descriptions.

1. A _____ shaped nose.

2. Red hair that _____ .

3. A voice that sounded like _____ .

4. Lips that _____ .

5. He wore a _____ jacket that

looked _____ .

6. The child's skin smelled like_____ .

7. The old man's eyes were _____ and

_____ .

8. Karen _____ into the classroom,

her shoulders _____

_____ ,

her face _____ .

9. The dog was _____ with around its ears. His fur was and .

10. The man had the face of a _____ .

Describing a Character

Use the chart below to brainstorm descriptions of a real or imaginary person. Use *specific details*. For example, rather than simply saying "He has blue eyes," a better description could be "He has eyes like pale blue marbles."

   Then use the chart to write a paragraph describing the person. Afterwards, share your description with a friend. Find out if you have painted a clear and interesting picture.

Face Shape	Height/Weight/Age
Eyes	Gait/Posture
Nose	Arms/Hands
Mouth	Legs/Feet
Hair	Style of Dress
Skin	Voice

Judging a Character by His Cover

A writer uses physical description not only to give the reader a mental picture but also to offer clues to the character's personality. For example, a grumpy person might be described as "wearing a permanent frown."

Here is an example of this type of description from *Incident at Hawk's Hill* by Allan Eckert (Little, Brown). The Newbery Honor book is about a young frontier boy who is "adopted" by a wild badger.

> *Burton was a very large man with a massive chest and huge hands. A dense, untrimmed black beard covered the lower portion of his face and his brows seemed abnormally bushy. Without the distracting influence of the beard and brows his nose might have been somewhat too big for his face and his chin too weak, but now there was a kind of unkept ruggedness to his countenance that one might well have expected of the frontier type that this fur trader was. He was a man who caused discomfort in those around him because his eyes never really met those of the person to whom he was talking. It gave the disconcerting impression of shiftiness, insincerity.*

1. What word does the author use to desribe Burton's chest? _____. What do you think the word means? _____. Check your guess by using the dictionary.

2. What do you think the phrase "unkept ruggedness to his countenance" means?_____
Check the words in the dictionary.

3. Which characteristic of Burton "caused discomfort in those around him"?_____

4. This characteristic gave a "*disconcerting* impression of *shiftiness* and *insincerity*." What do you think the italicized words mean?

_____

_____

Check your ideas with a classmate. Then verify answers with the dictionary.

Your Turn

Write a sentence that reveals something about a person's character through how they look or act. For example, Greg is shy. *When he was called on in class, or tried talking to a new girl, Greg's mouth would go dry and his tongue grow thick.*

1. The dog is playful. _____

_____

_____

2. Mr. Riley is a nervous man. _____

_____

_____

3. My aunt Sarah is an extremely busy person. _____

_____

_____

4. My baby sister is mischievious. _____

_____

_____

5. Randy is very enthusiastic about books and reading. ____

_____

_____

6. Our principal, Mrs. Evans, makes everyone feel welcome. ____

_____

_____

Colorful Characters

How do writers help us get to know the characters? You have seen how writers use direct description to describe a character's looks, personality, and background. Have you heard of the saying "Actions speak louder than words"? Another way writers help us learn about the characters is through their *actions*. Showing the character's personality rather than telling is usually a more interesting method of characterization.

Let's take a look at an example from *From the Mixed-Up Files of Mrs. Basil E. Frankweiler* by E. L. Konigsburg. The main character, 12-year-old Claudia, is planning a runaway adventure to the Metropolitan Museum of Art in New York City. What do you learn about Claudia's personality from this paragraph?

> *Claudia loved the city because it was elegant; it was important; and busy. The best place in the world to hide. She studied maps and the Tourguide book of the American Automobile Association and reviewed every field trip her class had ever taken. She made a specialized geography course for herself. There were even some pamphlets about the museum around the house, which she quietly researched.*

From one paragraph, the reader gets the impression that Claudia is curious, a planner, resourceful, and perhaps clever. The author *showed* this through Claudia's *actions*.

YOUR TURN

Use actions to describe a greedy and selfish person. (Do not use these words in the paragraph.)

_____

_____

_____

_____

_____

_____

Colorful Characters

How does a writer help us get to know the characters? Think about meeting a new teacher on the first day at school. The way he talks and what he says gives you clues to his personality. If he cracks a lot of jokes, you might think he has a sense of humor. Similarly, in books, the character's personality is often revealed through what he says.

In Jon Hassler's novel, *Four Miles to Pinecone*, the main character, Tommy, received an F in English class. After school, he meets with his English teacher, Mr. Singleton, to discuss the failing grade.

"Thomas," he said, "I know why you're here. You are less than satisfied with your grade."

"I'm in a state of shock," I said.

"All is not lost, Thomas. Pull up a desk and be seated. We shall talk. Nothing is hopeless."

"That's what I came to hear," I said. I sat down.

"Hope is a thing with feathers that perches in the soul." Mr Singleton is forever quoting dead poets....

"Mr. Singleton," I said, "I deserve better than an F in English. I did great on all your tests. I know everything you teach, and here you flunk me. How can you get away with that?"

I was coming on strong. His smile faded.

"Please do not question my judgment," he said. "Now it's true that you know a great deal about what I teach, but you have one great weakness—one vast flaw—in an otherwise adequate mentality."

"What's that?"

"You lack perseverance, my good young man."

"What's that?"

"Perseverance is another word for handing in assignments. Would you care to estimate the number of written assignments you failed to hand in during the year?"...

What can you tell about Mr. Singleton just from the above conversation?

_____

_____

_____

Your Turn

What a character says, and the *way* it is said, helps the reader get to know the character. Try imagining a different teacher in place of Mr. Singleton. How would this teacher's response to Tommy differ? Rewrite the scene by changing the teacher's words to show a different personality.

_____

_____

_____

_____

_____

_____

_____

_____

_____

_____

_____

_____

_____

_____

_____

_____

_____

_____

_____

_____

_____

_____

Dazzling Dialogue

Actual talk or conversation in writing is called *dialogue*. This is an important special effect. Clear, interesting dialogue brings the story and characters to life. Here are some tips to help you write better dialogue.

- *Check your tag lines.* The reader needs to know which character is speaking. A tag line is a couple of words or a phrase that tells you who is speaking.

    "What's that noise?" *Jerry asked.*
    "It's coming from the basement," *Paul whispered.*
- *Avoid using adjectives, adverbs, and fancy verbs to describe the tone of voice.*

    "What's that noise?" *Jerry asked nervously.*
    "It's coming from the basement," *Paul whispered softly.*
- *Combine action with dialogue.*

    Jerry's palms were sweating. "What's that noise?"
    Paul stopped to listen. "It's coming from the basement," he whispered.
- *You do not always need a tag line. Sometimes it is obvious who is speaking.*

    Paul and Jerry crept down the dark hall. Suddenly, Jerry grabbed Paul's arm. "What's that noise?"
    Paul stopped to listen. "It's coming from the basement," he whispered.
    "We better get out of here."
    "Are you crazy? We just got here."
    "Paul, I'm not going to get in trouble."
    "Shh. Just listen for a moment."

Rules to Remember

1. Use a new paragraph each time you change speakers.
2. The actual words the character says go inside the quotation marks. ("Watch out!" Paul screamed. "Run!")
3. Use a comma before the tag line if the sentence would ordinarily end with a period. ("I'm leaving camp," Debbi announced.) Do not use a comma if the statement calls for a question mark or exclamantion mark. ("Why not?" asked Glen. "Because, I said so!" snapped his father.)

Creating Characters

Below are excerpts of terrific writing from young adult novels. After reading each quote, decide which method of characterization the author used: physical description, direct description, action, words, thoughts, or what others say.

*Darry is six-feet-two, and broad-shouldered and muscular....
He's got eyes that are like two pieces of pale blue-green ice.*
—The Outsiders *by S. E. Hinton*

---

*"Good afternoon, Miss Jackson," the teacher's voice, thick with
sarcasm, followed her to her seat.... The teacher's voice rose
sharply: "It seems to me that if you had to honor us with your
presence today, you could at least have been preparing yourself to come to class looking presentable."*
—The Friends *by Rosa Guy*

---

*Another thing about Gloria. She had this habit of saying things
to make you ask a question. She would walk up to you and say
something like, "Well, I guess it had to happen sometime."*
—The Young Landlords *by Walter Dean Myers*

---

*How could he have lived all his years without knowing that he
was the biggest coward in the world, he wondered, he, the son
of the bravest of men?... He would have to learn to hide it
until, he learned to be brave.*
—Shadow of a Bull *by Maia Wojciechowska*

---

*Gabool the Wild ruled the seas, he was the dread Lord of Ter-
ramort Island, King of the Searats, Warlord of all Rodent Cor-
sairs, Captain of Captain. No creature alive was a fiercer
fighter than Gabool.*
—Mariel of Redwall *by Brian Jacques*

Mrs. Rachel was sitting at her window, keeping a sharp eye on everything that passed, from brooks and children up, and that if she noticed anything odd or out of place she would never rest until she had ferreted out the whys and wherefores thereof.
—Anne of Green Gables *by Lucy Maude Montgomery*

Your Turn

Write a description of a person using each method of characterization.

1. Physical Description

_____

_____

2. Direct Description

_____

_____

3. Action

_____

_____

4. Words

_____

_____

5. Thoughts

_____

_____

6. What Others Say

_____

_____

Character Change

Book/Story _____

PHYSICAL DESCRIPTION: Hair, eyes, manner of dress, gestures, age voice, etc.

ACTIONS: List significant things the character has done. How does he or she treat others?

PERSONALITY: Think of adjectives that describe the character's personality. Then prove it. Examples of characteristics are stubborn, lazy, protective, joker, loving, moody, etc.

ADJECTIVE: _____   PROOF: _____
_____
_____

GOALS:

OBSTACLES:

CHANGES DURING THE STORY

BEFORE: AFTER:

SIGNIFICANT QUOTES FROM CHARACTER:

YOUR OPINION OF AUTHOR'S CHARACTER DEVELOPMENT:

What Happens Next?

"This book was great! I couldn't put it down." Every author hopes to hear these words. Writers use several different special effects to make the reader keep turning the pages. What are some ways writers can keep the reader's attention?

_____

_____

Good writers will have you saying, "I wonder what will happen next?" *Creating curiosity* is a special effect. A writer can create curiousity by withholding information from the reader. Let's look at an example from James Baldwin, a major voice of black America in the 1950s and 1960s. Here is the beginning of his short story, "Sonny's Blues":

I read about it in the paper, in the subway, on my way to work. I read it, and I couldn't believe it, and I read it again. Then perhaps I just stared at it, at the newsprint spelling out his name, spelling out the story. I stared at it in the swinging lights of the subway care, and in the faces and bodies of the people, and in my own face, trapped in the darkness which roared outside.

1. What question comes to mind as you read this?

_____

2. What do you suppose the narrator is reading about and what clue

does the author give? _____

The author continues to create curiosity in the second paragraph.

It was not to be believed and I kept telling myself that, as I walked from the subway station to the high school. And at the same time I couldn't doubt it. I was scared, scared for Sonny.

3. Now what question comes to mind? _____

_____

Watch how the author offers clues but still continues to make the reader more curious in the following paragraph.

He became real to me again. A great block of ice got settled in my belly and kept melting there slowly all day long, while I taught my classes algebra. It was a special kind of ice. It kept melting, sending trickles of ice water all up and down my veins, but it never got less. Sometimes it hardened and seemed to expand until I felt my guts were going to come spilling out or that I was going to choke or scream. This would alway be at a moment when I was remembering some specific thing Sonny had once said or done.

4. Based on the information in the first two paragraphs of the story, what relationship do you think the narrator and Sonny had?

_____

_____

_____

5. By now, we are yearning to know just who Sonny is and what he did. What do you imagine the narrator might have read in the newspaper that was so shocking? _____

_____

_____

_____

Your Turn

Write a paragraph that creates a feeling of curiosity.

_____

_____

_____

_____

_____

_____

_____

_____

_____

_____

_____

Sizzling Suspense

Another special effect for making the reader want to know more is *creating suspense*. This is also known as *story tension*. Every story must have some tension. Stories with a lot of tension are called *suspense stories,* such as Lois Duncan's *Stranger with My Face.* Just like a suspenseful movie may have you "sitting on the edge of your seat," a suspenseful book will have you turning pages.

Gary Paulsen is a master at writing survival stories such as *Hatchet, The Crossing,* and *Tracker.* Gary's childhood was marked by poverty, loneliness, and family problems. His life experiences as a farmer, beaver trapper, dogsledder, woodsman, rancher, truck river, and sailor are captured in his thrilling books. Here is an excerpt from *Woodsong,* a true account of his years living in the woods. In this scene, Paulsen is burning trash in the wilderness when he encounters a bear attracted to the burning food scraps.

I have made many mistakes in my life, and will probably make many more, but I hope never to throw a stick at a bear again.

In one rolling motion—the muscles seemed to move within the skin so fast that I couldn't take half a breath—he turned and came for me. Close. I could smell his breath and see the red around the sides of his eyes. Close on me he stopped and raised on his back legs and hung over me, his forelegs and paws hanging down, weaving back and forth gently as he took his time and decided whether or not to tear my head off.

I could not move, would not have time to react. I knew I had nothing to say about it. One blow would break my neck. Whether I lived or died depended on him, on his thinking, on his ideas about me—whether I was worth the bother or not.

How does Paulsen manage to create *suspense* in these three paragraphs?

_____

_____

Here are some tips for creating story tension or suspense.

1. Put the character in a dangerous situation.
2. Do not tell the reader everything at once.
3. Keep a secret from the reader and let it unfold slowly.

4. Give your character an important decision to make.

5. Give your character a goal and make the reader care whether or not the character attains it.

6. Use sensory words, strong verbs, and specific nouns to describe a suspenseful scene.

Which one of these 6 tips do you think Gary Paulsen used in the excerpt of *Woodsong?*

Your Turn

Write a suspenseful scene by using one or two of the above six tips. Remember, you do not have to show the outcome.

_____

_____

_____

_____

_____

_____

_____

_____

_____

_____

_____

_____

_____

_____

Revising

Reread your writing. Did you paint a picture? Did you *show* instead of *tell?*

A Writer's Special Effects

Purpose: To help readers learn to recognize a writer's special effects and unlock the secrets to creating a sensational story

Discussion Starter: What are special effects?

Say: Movie directors sometimes use special effects to grab your attention or to amaze the audience. Sometimes, special effects help a movie seem more real, magical, or scary. Special effects can turn a person's face into a monster, make people fly, and make animals talk. Books have special effects, too, though they may not jump out at you, as in the movies. A writer can use special effects to make a story suspenseful, funny, or sad. A good writer can make you so absorbed that you forget where you are. A good writer paints a picture with words.

Direction to Students: Think about a story that you have read or heard that really captured your attention. Write something about this memorable story.

Next: Ask students to share what they have written with a classmate. Did any students select the same story?

Alternate plan: For students who cannot think of a story example, try soliciting a news story, movie, or family tale.

Painting a Picture

Lesson: Details

Say or Write: Good writers are artists of words. They strive to paint a mental picture for the reader. Painting a picture with words is more than just good description. The writer must make the readers feel as if they are *there*. Writers use different special effects to achieve this goal. To write well, one must be a good observer.

Activity:

1. Look around the room where you are right now. Jot down words that describe what you see.
2. Now compare lists with your classmates. How are your observations similar or different?
3. Now go back over your list. What details could you add to paint a clearer picture? Suppose you noticed a pile of books. Are they paperback? Tattered? Thick? Brand new?

Write: SIZE, SHAPE, COLOR, TEXTURE

Say: These are categories we can use to describe objects in our world. Look around the room again. Use these categories to expand the description of your surroundings.

Sharpening Observation Skills

To write vivid description, students must have the words and the power of observation. The following game is a fun way to increase observation and descriptive vocabulary.

    1. Collect a variety of small objects such as a watch, flower, plate, rock, doll, and candle.

    2. Divide the class into groups of two to five. Students need paper and pens. Give one object to each group.

    3. Allow students to briefly handle the object. Then give them 15 seconds to write down specific words that describe the object.

    4. When time is up, each member of the group reads his or her list aloud. The other students cross off words on their lists that have been mentioned. Sudents score one point for any word on their list that did not appear on another member's list.

    5. Change objects and continue the game.

Moving with Words

After students have had practice replacing weak verbs and have read examples of writers desribing action, ask them to write a paragraph describing an observed action such as a car chase, a dance, a baseball game, a horse race, a parade, or a building of a tree house.

Colorful Characters

Say: A writer's job is to tell a good story. Along the way, the writer must also create interesting characters who come alive on the printed page. The writer must make the reader care about what happens to the main character. By the end of the book, the reader should feel like the character is a close friend.

You may remember the colorful characters in E. B. White's famous book, *Charlotte's Web*. Millions of children have grown to love Wilbur the pig and his wise spider friend, Charlotte. E. B. White used his "special effects" to create interesting and distinct characters.

Ask: What memorable characters have you met through reading? Can you think of ways that writers help you get to know the characters in a story? (List responses on the board or chart.)

Describing a Character

Ask: What are some ways a writer can help you get to know the characters in a story?

Do: List the students' ideas on the board. They will probably focus first on *physical description*. What is included in physical description?

Do: Collect a variety of photographs of people from magazines. Have students work in groups to list pertinent physical descriptions.

Do: Use excerpts to highlight excellent use of physical description. Have students pick out what aspects of a character's appearance are described, such as body shape, clothing, voice, hair texture, and gait.

Resources:

To Kill a Mockingbird by Harper Lee. See description of the new teacher, Miss Cunningham.

A Christmas Carol by Charles Dickens. See initial description of Scrooge.

The Outsiders by S. E. Hinton. See initial descriptions of the gang members, particularly Darry and Johnny.

Child of the Owl by Lawrence Yep. See description in Chapter One of Morey, the old musician.

Creating Characters

Write: "My characters always take shape first; they wander around my mind looking for something to do. I know I'm ready to put them in a story when an ending comes to mind. The ending always comes first." —S. E. Hinton

Ask: What do you think the author means? Why do you suppoe she thinks of the ending first? If you have read any of Hinton's books, what can you recall about the characters?

Dazzling Dialogue

Learning to write dialogue can enhance reading comprehension. Through practice and example, students build an awareness of the function and form of dialogue, adding insight to their reading.

Activities:

1. Train students to listen to speech. Play a videotape of a sit-com or a movie scene. Darken or cover the screen so students focus only on the dialogue. Can the dialogue stand on its own? Why or why not? How is it different from real-life speech? From dialogue in books?
2. Read aloud (or listen to a recording) of old radio plays such as "Sorry, Wrong Number" by Louise Fletcher (Radio Reruns, Toronto, 1980).
3. Have students work in twos and threes to act out a dialogue scene from a novel.
4. Have students search for examples of dialogue that: (a) reveal past events, (b) reveal something about a character, (c) reveal new information, (d) break up narrative, (e) create a dramatic scene, and (f) create a humorous scene.
5. Have students practice writing a dialogue for specific situations, such as a mother revealing a past secret to her child, two friends planning a surprise party for a third, and a boy and a girl at their first school dance.
6. Working in pairs, let students have a 10-minute written conversation. How does it differ from ordinary talk? From story dialogue? Have them revise the conversation and add narrative to creat an interesting scene.
7. Have students write a dialogue that shows conflict. Consider ideas from real life at home or in school.
8. Have artistic students create their own comic strips. Photocopy comic strips without the dialogue. Have students fill in the captions.

Tattle Tales

Discussion Starter: How would you describe your sister, brother, or best friends?

Say: We can learn about someone through what others say about him or her. In the same way, a writer may reveal things about a character through another character's eyes.

Let's look at an example from *The Pigman* by Paul Zindel. Lorraine is describing her good friend John.

The one big difference between John and me, besides the fact that he's a boy and I'm a girl, is I have compassion. Not that he really doesn't have any compassion, but he'd be the last one on earth to show it. He pretends he doesn't care about anything in the world, and he's always ready with some outrageous remark, but if you ask me, any real hostility he has is directed against himself.

Follow-Up: Brainstorm character traits such as stubborness, generosity, and laziness. Then have students categorize them into positive and negative traits. Which traits could fit in both categories? Ask students to write a short description of someone they know, focusing on one or two character traits. Encourage them to use examples in actions and words.

A Penny for Your Thoughts

Say: Another way writers help us get to know a character is through his or her thoughts. This technique gives the reader a window into the character's mind and heart. Listening to a character's thoughts also helps us see how a character changes throughout the story.

Activities:

1. Ask students to find examples of characters thinking to themselves. What information is gleaned?
2. Have students write interior monologues for fairy tale characters such as Cinderella, Goldilocks, and the Big Bad Wolf. Let classmates guess the character.
3. Have students write interior monologues for a fictional character that worries too much or is very sensitive or conceited.

References

Atwell, Nancie. (1987). *In the Middle: Writing, Reading, and Learning with Adolescents.* Portsmouth, NH: Boynton/Cook Heinemann.

Graves, Donald, & Hansen, Jane. (1983). The author's chair. *Language Arts, 60,* 176–183.

Krieger, Evelyn. (1992). The story behind the story. *The Journal of Reading, 35,* 498–499.

Lightman, Alan. (1994). My back pages. *The Boston Globe,* Section B, April 24, p. 16.

Children's Literature

Baldwin, James. (1965). Sonny Blues, in James Baldwin (Ed.), *Going to Meet the Man*. New York: Dial.

Bradbury, Ray. (1960). All summer in a day, in *A Medicine for Melancholy*. New York: Bantam.

Eckert, Allan. (1971). *Incident at Hawk's Hill*. Boston: Little, Brown.

Fox, Paula. (1968). *The Stone-Faced Boy*. Englewood Cliffs, NJ: Bradbury.

Guy, Rosa. (1973). *The Friends*. New York: Holt.

Hassler, Jon. (1977). *Four Miles to Pinecone*. New York: Warne.

Konigsburg, E. L. (1967). *The Mixed-Up Files of Mrs. Basil E. Frankweiler*. New York: Atheneum.

Lipsyte, Robert. (1967). *The Contender*. New York: Harper and Row.

London, Jack. (1986). To build a fire, in *Novels & Stories by Jack London*. New York: Bantam.

Paulsen, Gary. (1990). *Woodsong*. New York: Bradbury.

Steinbeck, John. (1956). *The Long Valley*. New York: Viking.

Yep, Laurence. (1977). *Child of the Owl*. New York: Harper and Row.

Zindel, Paul. (1968). *The Pigman*. New York: Harper and Row.

Resources for Setting the Scene

Bellairs, John. (1973). *The House with a Clock on Its Wall*. New York: Dial. (Magical house)

George, Jean Craighead. (1972). *Julie of the Wolves*. New York: Harper and Row. (Alaskan tundra)

Harvey, B. (1986). *My Prairie Year*. New York: Holiday House.

Paulsen, Gary. (1988). *The Island*. New York: Dell. (Wisconsin countryside)

Pearce, Philippa. (1958). *Tom's Midnight Garden*. Oxford: Oxford University Press. (English countryside garden)

Salisbury, Graham. (1992). *Blue Skin of the Sea*. New York: Delacorte. (Hawaiian fishing village)

Wheatley, Nadia, & Rawlins, Donna. (1992). *My Place*. Brooklyn, NY: Kane/Miller. (A 200-year history of an Australian coastal town told chronologically through narratives of young children living there. Picture book.)

Yolen, Jane. (1988). *The Devil's Arithmetic*. New York: Viking Kestrel. (Poland during World War II)

4

Reading, Writing, and Revising

I enjoy cutting, reordering, developing, shaping, polishing my drafts.
Never have I failed to make a text better by my revision and editing.
I cannot say that has always been true when others have revised
and edited my texts, but it is true when I have practiced surgery
on my own words.

—Donald M. Murray (1990)

I can remember my elementary school days where I was forced to copy compositions over until they were "perfect." Thank goodness I learned to type in high school and discovered correction fluid. By then, I was a budding writer who understood the value and messiness of revision. Several years later, I converted to using the word processor and, today, I can't imagine a writing life without it.

If your classroom is without a computer (our school was fortunate to have a lab), I encourage you to solicit school administrators or outside sources for funding to purchase as many as possible. The computer is a vital tool in any school writing program. Students no longer have to worry about laborious or messy handwriting. Young writers can delete a paragraph or move it around the text in a matter of seconds. Spell-check and thesaurus programs help with editing. Creative writing software programs can engage reluctant writers and free the teacher to hold writing conferences with individual students. Students with compatible home computers can take home their disks to work on.

So, while revising may be a less painful task than in yesteryear, students who print out first drafts on the laser printer may be misled by the professional package. Young writers must not only know how to identify errors and weak spots but they also must *want* to correct and revise them. With the popularity of the process writing approach—think, write, rewrite, edit—most students come to middle school with the basics of revision. I find, however, that students rely on the teacher as editor. They want me to tell them what to say and how to say it. (This is true for spelling and grammar as well.) This should not be surprising, as teachers have traditionally played editor and evaluator of student writing.

To assist students in their revisions when a computer is not available, try creating an attractive and professional-looking revision station equipped with correction fluid, stick-on note pads, colored pens, paper, scissors, glue, erasers, a thesaurus, dictionaries, writing guides, and checklists.

Ask your students these questions:

1. What is the difference between revision and editing?
2. How does one know when the writing is revised enough?
3. Can a piece of writing ever be perfect? How would you decide?

Answers to such questions can offer insight into their understanding of the revision and editing process.

Revision can be a process of self-discovery. For this to happen, the act of revising must come mainly from the writer. The teacher/editor can give impressions and suggestions, but in the end, it is the writer who must pull it all together and make his or her words sing. Inspiring students to rewrite, rework, and revise their writing involves showing them how real writers approach revision.

> *I learned to write when I accepted that the first writing, a draft, was only that—a beginning, a reaching, an approximation of what I wanted. (Mazer, 1992)*

In Their Own Words

When author Walter Dean Myers visited our junior high school, he told the students how much time he spent on revision. He told them about his rejection slips. He told them that writing, good writing, is a lot of hard work. Then he showed the youngsters his stack of published books.

Over the years, I have noticed that my students approach their own writing with a different perspective after listening to the "shoptalk" of their favorite authors. (For more on author visits, see Chapter 5.) Simply reading quotes from writers can also shape students' ideas about revision. One of my favorites is from Isaac Bashevis Singer.

> *The main rule of a writer is never pity your manuscript. If you see something is no good, throw it away and begin again. A lot of writers have failed because they have too much pity. They have already worked so much, they cannot just throw it away. But I say that the wastepaper basket is a writer's best friend. My wastepaper basket is on a steady diet. (Singer 1990, p. 187)*

I often use a quote at the beginning of a mini-lesson or when students are struggling with a certain aspect of revision such as deleting unnecessary words. Good sources for such quotes are *Shoptalk: Learning to Write with Writers* by Donald Murray, *How Writers Write* by Pamela Lloyd, and *Speaking for Ourselves* by Donald Gallo.

Another way to demonstrate the value of revision is to show students a real manuscript get a makeover. I have used drafts of my published articles. Students note the changes I made and why I made them. Then they compare the published piece to my final draft to check for the editor's touches. My students are always surprised by these revisions: "But you're a teacher!"

You need not be published to achieve this effect. Sharing revisions you made in everyday writing, such as a letter to parents, demonstrates how adults work at making writing clear. Inviting a news reporter or book editor to visit your classroom is another way to show the importance of revision in real writing.

An editor of a small publishing house spoke to my Famous Author classes on the publication process. She distributed copies of a children's picture book manuscript and then elicited student opinions. "Would it make a good book?" the editor asked. Most said it would not and gave valid reasons. The students were pleased to learn that the editor agreed with them.

Next, the class looked at a manuscript that was accepted for publication. However, they were told that this manuscript needed work. The editor discussed specific criteria for children's picture books and then asked the students to make changes and comments. After discussing this first draft and the suggested revisions, the editor passed out copies of the published book for students to compare with the draft. She asked them to study the accompanying illustrations as well.

What made this meaningful, real-life lesson even more powerful was that the published author was a 12-year-old girl—Alexandra Wright—who attended our school. Her beautiful book is *Will We Miss Them? Endangered Species* (Charlesbridge, 1991), followed by *At Home in the Tide Pool* (Charlesbridge, 1993).

The Language of Revision

Once students understand that real writers revise, they are more likely to view revision as a chance to make good writing into great writing, rather than a teacher's torture. As Newbery Award writer Katherine Paterson (1981) concludes, "Where else in life can spilled milk be transformed into ice cream?"

I like to liven up the teaching of revision by using catchy phrases to describe the process. Repeating these phrases during writing conferences, class lessons, as well as writing them on student drafts, reinforces the underlying concept. Add a dose of enthusiasm and watch student motivation grow. Copy the next page for your students.

> *To revise is to see with new eyes. A problem passage can become a strength, a dead word can come alive, and a confusing thought can spark a brilliant idea. Seen this way, revision isn't a chore; it's a second chance. (Hutchinson, 1991)*

Editing

> *Early in the school year I use a mini lesson to explain that writers edit because they want the writing to invite reading and to mean to others what they intend. (Atwell, 1987)*

Showing students why punctuation and grammar make sense is a more effective teaching tool than spewing rules at them. (Ever wonder why we have to teach the apostrophe rules *every* year from fourth through twelfth grade?) As teacher/writer Nancie Atwell (1987) says, "I show kids why punctuation was invented—essentially to show readers what to do with their voices—and how the different marks work to that effect." Perhaps teachers feel more comfortable with a scope and sequence list of skills to be covered during the school year. Perhaps it is easier to say, "Now we are going to learn about comma usage." Drill, skill, and test. Once upon a time, I used this approach until I realized I was reteaching the same skills time and time again. In most instances, the skills did not transfer. Furthermore, the drill/skill approach seemed a disservice to those students who had mastered that particular skill. Finally, frequent use of grammar worksheets and lessons turned youngsters off to writing. Students of high school age may be more receptive and better able to transfer grammar rules to their own writing, but most elementary and middle school students find such isolated grammar exercises boring and irrelevant. Keep in mind that students generate plenty of bad writing that is grammatically correct.

Many parents (as well as teachers and administrators) still cling to the notion that memorizing grammar rules is essential for learning to write well. I often hear the "good-old days" speech from parents about how they were forced to diagram sentences and are thankful for it today. "The problem with kids today is that they don't know grammar!" is a common refrain.

Perhaps you, too, have felt the futility of assigning weekly lessons from grammar books. Perhaps you are frustrated by how little improvement you see in your students' writing. Or maybe you wonder why you are still teaching period usage in

Let's Talk Revision!

Time for surgery.	Delete unnecessary words and redundancies.
Time for the Ps.	Proofread, punctuate, and polish.
Paint the picture.	Add description and imagery.
Set the scene.	Describe where and when the event happens.
Make every word count.	Don't add unnecessary words.
Revive your verbs.	Get rid of weak verbs and verbs of being.
Use your senses.	Use sensory words and details to describe.
Grab the reader.	Revise the opening.
Stay on the road.	Make your point and stick to it.
Say it again.	Ask yourself: How can I say this more clearly?
Smooth it.	Make the sentence clearer.
Tighten up.	Use two words instead of four. Be concise.
Cure "adjective-itis."	Don't pile on the adjectives. Try figurative language.
Name that noun.	Use specific nouns that conjure an image.
Tell me more!	Add details and information.
Unscramble, please.	Fix awkward sentences.
Show me!	Show it; don't tell it.

the eighth grade. Today, teachers are often advised to teach skills in context. The notion is fairly simple: Teach students a particular skill based on specific errors made in the context of their own writing. Makes sense, doesn't it? I can just hear you saying, "Sure it sounds great in theory, but how can I make this work in my classroom of 25 kids of varying abilities?" Try these mini-lessons.

Mini-Lessons

Lucy Calkins (1986) first wrote about mini-lessons in her wonderful book, *The Art of Teaching Writing*. The basic idea is that the teacher presents a brief lesson on a skill that students are lacking or will need to use that day. For example, suppose your students are working on writing short fiction. You notice that many students have difficulty with quotation marks in dialogue. So before students sit down to write and revise, you give a class mini-lesson on dialogue.

Teacher: Before we begin working on our stories today, I'd like to bring something to your attention. I've noticed that many of you have used dialogue in your stories. That's a great way to make characters come alive as well as move the story forward. However, if you want the reader to understand who is talking, you need to know the correct way to use quotation marks. Let's look at an example from Mark's story.

Mini-lessons are painless. They help focus students' attention on a skill they need at that moment. They can be invaluable for teaching the editing process.

Record Keeping

Teaching skills in context requires teachers to be good record keepers. You will need to know what skills students need and what skills they know. As you read your students' work and confer with them about their writing, jot down problem areas in a special notebook. You can use this suggestion for writing techniques, revision, and grammar. Here is a sample for editing.

> —John, Feb. 10, Essay, unclear use of pronoun references.
> —Cindy, Feb. 10, Short story, inconsistent voice; interchanges *she* and *I*.

When students receive feedback on an problem area while in the process of writing, they are more likely to internalize the correct way. This "teaching on the spot" method is more effective than taking the paper away, editing it yourself, and then returning it a few days later.

Perhaps you wish to move toward teaching editing and grammar skills in context but worry that parents will object. You are right to be concerned. Parents are leery of unfamiliar teaching practices. They want proof and specifics. As Atwell (1987) says,

> *They want to know that their children are learning what students in an English class are supposed to be learning, and in my editing conference journal I can show exactly what their children are learning in the context of pieces of writing over the days and weeks of the writing workshop.*

Atwell goes on to describe the format of her well-organized editing journal that contains a few pages for each student. She not only records skills that were taught but also skills a student uses correctly. Students also keep their own lists of "Things That I Can Do as a Writer."

If you find the editing journal approach a bit too open ended, then try typing a list of skills you would like your students to learn by the end of the term. Turn this into a chart by adding student names at the top. Check off the appropriate space after a student has demonstrated competence in that area.

The Pains and Pleasures of Peer Editing

The idea of peer editing, a student critiquing and editing another student's writing, came in vogue with the evolution of process writing and whole language teaching. Rearch suggests that peer editing can improve reading and writing in addition to fostering cooperative and active learning (Harp, 1988). The theories behind peer editing make sense and may be appealing to teachers searching for ways to get students involved in the revision and editing process.

However, in my experience and that of many teachers I have met, the reality of peer editing is another story. One teacher told me that after trying peer editing, he felt it was like "the blind leading the blind." Since peer editing sounds so simple, teachers may jump on the bandwagon without really examining the method beforehand. They have their students exchange essays, instruct them to write comments and suggestions to the author, and then incorporate their classmate's critique into the final draft of the essay.

The results are often disappointing. Students may be ruthless in their comments ("This essay stinks!"); they may have little to say ("I like this essay.") or they may have too much to say. To complicate matters, the writer may feel insulted, intimidated, embarrassed, or may simply disagree with the peer editor's comments.

Finally, when it comes to the mechanical stage of editing, which one might assume is more straightforward, the teacher still encounters problems. Some students are terrible spellers and will not catch errors. Middle school students may be able to sense something is wrong with a sentence but lack the grammatical vocabulary to pinpoint the problem. I must admit, I was initially sold on the idea of peer editing in the classroom. I have not given up on it, either. What I learned is this: To reap the rewards, one must be willing to put in the time to prepare and train the students. Finally, the students need time to practice peer editing. This is a messy and chaotic process, but the end result can be beautiful—students taking on responsibility, working cooperatively, practicing useful skills, reading with a critical eye, and writing with a sense of reader.

Consider the following six steps by Harp (1988) to more pleasurable peer editing:

1. *Build student understanding of the revision and editing process.*

2. *Gradually introduce the process of peer editing to your class.* I have asked students to volunteer their writing for class review. You can also use samples from previous years. Make copies for each student or use an overhead projector or computer disk. "Let's help Corrine to revise her essay," you might suggest. Then guide students through one aspect of the process, such as extraneous words or sentence order. As students learn more about revision, you can cover more ground with each sample text.

3. *Allow students to practice a specific revision skill using peer editing.* For example, if you have just taught a mini-lesson on ways to improve opening sentences, then have students pair up and comment on this only. Make sure students understand the focus. You might say, "Now you and your editor should exchange comments on the use of description."

4. *Continue to model the process and give students examples of the type of comments that are most helpful to their peers.* After students have learned to focus on spe-

cific features of revision, you might want them to give an overall impression of a student's work. For example, after Corrine reads her short story to the class, you might ask for reactions. If you first model this process to the whole class, as well as with individual students, they are more likely to offer insightful and specific comments that actually help the writer. Some teachers hang a poster that lists examples of such comments.

5. *State explicit guidelines for the peer editing process.* Teachers tell me they have management problems when using peer editing. To avoid this, make sure the steps, procedures, and behavioral expectations are clear at the onset.

6. *Strongly encourage students to use the feedback in revising their writing.* Not only do we want students to be able to identify weaknesses and errors in writing but we also want them to be able to incorporate this knowledge into their own work. One of the important lessons of peer editing is that hearing the reactions of our readers can help us become better writers. Young people are, by nature, egocentric. Discovering how their words are received by others is a valuable part of learning to write with a sense of reader. The student writer needs time to digest and utilize the peer comments.

When I introduce the idea of peer editing to my students, I like to tell them about a creative writing course I took in college. There were only 15 students in the class. The professor asked us to distribute photocopies of our short stories to each class member. When a story was introduced, the professor elicited feedback on the language, form, characterization, dialogue, and so on. There was one rule: The author of the work under discussion could not speak.

I tell my class how shy and carefully guarded I was about my writing. However, I aspired to publication, and, as my professor said, "If writing is to be communication, then you must find out what you have communicated." I describe to my students how difficult it was to listen to the class members, strangers really, critique my precious words. My immediate reaction was to defend or explain myself, which I was not permitted to do. (How dare they tell me to change that brilliant ending!) Though I did not agree with everything that was said, I gained valuable perspective and insight. The blinders that the solitary act of writing creates were lifted. The lesson became clear. Opening our eyes to what the reader sees and our ears to what the reader hears and our hearts to what the reader feels, though scary and intimidating, allows us to grow as writers.

A sentence should contain no unnecessary words, a paragraph no unnecessary sentences, for the same reason that a drawing should have no unnecessary lines and a machine no unnecessary parts. (Strunk & White, 1959)

RECIPE FOR A COMPOSITION

1 delicious beginning
1 cup of clear thoughts
A handful of details
1 tsp. of tasty adjectives
2 tsp. of verbs
1 strong ending

Arrange ingredients in a sensible order. Stir with imagination. Bake until the middle is well done. Let sit for a day before eating. Add seasoning if needed.

Me? An Author?

In elementary school I began to make books. My first books, made in kindergarten, were illustrated ABC and counting books. These one-of-a-kind limited editions drew rave reviews from family and friends and were given as gifts on all occasions. (Bryan, 1986)

Middle school kids love to talk. They like to gossip, tease, joke around, and hang out with friends. They write notes to each other behind our backs and chat on the phone for hours each night. Why not capitalize on this energy and interest in the classroom?

Helping students find avenues for their writing outside the teacher/student format can motivate, inspire, and reward even the most reluctant writers. After all, if we are going to preach the importance of good writing skills and proper grammar, we ought to show the youngsters the payoff in real life. When students have opportunities to write for a broader audience, they become attuned to the power of writing as a communication form. Seeing one's name in print and having one's words make a difference is an exciting prospect for young adolescents.

Classroom Publishing

Over the years, I have observed that my students work a little harder at their writing when they know it will be read by their peers. Perhaps they care less about how I view their spelling, grammar, and handwriting, or maybe they have little invested in impressing me (other than for a decent grade). Whatever the reason, I am willing to bet you will find this, too. I remember one year after a unit on suspense and ghost stories, I asked the children if they would like to take a stab at writing their own. My proposition was greeted with minimal enthusiasm. When I suggested that they try to scare their classmates with a good story, the interest level perked up considerably. Young people want their voices to be heard by someone other than their teachers whose role is too often as judges. Here are a number of ways to broaden your students' audience through classroom publishing.

Thematic Anthologies

After studying a particular topic, genre, or writing form, students work on submitting their best piece to the class anthology. For example, my students' final drafts of their tales of terror were typed, photocopied, and compiled in a bound book that became a part of our classroom library. Attractive portfolios containing plastic-covered pages can be purchased at office supply stores. Looseleaf binders or handmade covers are another alternative. Use calligraphy, stencils, or stick-on letters for book cover design.

A more ambitious (perhaps once a year) publishing project is a themed anthology each student may keep. This requires more time and assistance for photocopying, collating, and binding. Funds may be needed to cover costs. With desk-top publishing programs, computer graphics, and a laser printer, the quality of such projects can be quite professional.

My Reading Workshop students each selected their best work to include in our spring literary journal. The students were involved in designing a cover, collating pages, and using the binding machine supplied by our shop teacher. We planned an after-school publishing party to which each student invited parents, siblings, and friends.

Here are some topics we explored and wrote about in our classroom anthologies.

You're in Business   After reading about examples of entrepreneurship and learning business vocabulary—such as *market, start up,* and *overhead*—the class brainstormed ideas for student-run businesses. Teams of students worked together designing their own businesses. After studying examples of business proposals, students wrote their own then created a logo and an advertisement.

A School from Scratch   Students read about unique school programs and examples of educational reform. The class discussed the problems facing schools today. Students shared opinions on the positive and negative qualities in their school. Suggestions for improvement were offered. Discussion then focused on the goals of a school. This prepared them to fully consider the question: If you could design your dream school, what would it be like? The final project included a profile of their dream school, which included a philosophic statement, academic courses and objectives, schedule, special features, and physical setting.

Tales of Terror   Students read short stories samples from anthologies such as *Scary Tales to Tell in the Dark* by Alvin Schwartz (1981) then analyzed what special effects the authors used. Exercises in sensory writing and creating tension were given. The students exchanged ideas for scary situations and places before writing. (The challenge here was to clear the students' minds of TV and movie images.)

School Days   Memories of kindergarten and first grade were evoked through discussion and imagery exercises. Students learned techniques of "setting the scene" and read examples of school memories from literature selections (such as Harper Lee's *To Kill a Mockingbird)* before writing their own memories.

All About...   Youngsters love to be authorities. I asked each student to think of a skill, topic, game, activity, hobby, or sport that he or she could teach a friend about. Then I challenged them to put the information in writing. Next, they tested their piece for clarity and content by using partner editing, then revised as needed. The results were fascinating: Stamp collecting, downhill skiing, Irish step dancing, woodworking, life in Iran, the holiday of Kwanza, and asthma were covered.

Student Handbooks

One spring, my Reading Workshop students wrote a handbook for the sixth-graders who would enter junior high the following year. Each writer contributed a feature on topics such as making friends, the cafeteria, sports programs, and the school schedule. Copies of the handbook were distributed to all sixth-grade classrooms. My student authorities glowed upon receiving many compliments from teachers, students, and parents.

School Newspaper

One elective English course offered at our middle school was The Newspaper. As a final project, the students created a school newspaper and distributed it to the home-rooms. Features included teacher interviews, sports news, comics, editorials, and book reviews.

School Arts Journal

In 1990, our school media specialist and I recieved a grant from the Newton Schools Foundation to produce an intergenerational arts journal. We wanted to give students an opportunity to read, see, and appreciate the creative work of their peers. In addition, we wanted to recognize the artistic interests of our faculty and staff. A committee of students helped solicit creative writing and visual art and promoted the journal. We held a schoolwide contest to select a journal title and cover.

After several months of hard work, boxes of the bound *Rainbow* arrived in time for our publishing party, author signing, and journal sale. A class set of the journal was kept in the resource room for teachers to use in their English classes.

Student Books

Writing, illustrating, and binding their own books is fun and a wonderful learning experience for students. There are several resources that guide youngsters through the book-making process (see the end of this chapter). The possible types of bindings range from simple to complex. Those who feel inept at illustrating can collaborate with an artistic friend.

Each of my students wrote and revised a short work of fiction then divided the text into several pages and planned the illustrations. Published books included a dedication and an about-the-author page. Their efforts were celebrated with a publishing party. The colorful hardcover books displayed around the classroom inspired pride in us all.

Other Publishing Opportunities

In 1987, 14-year-old Stacy Chbosky of Pittsburgh, Pennsylvania, won a publishing contract with Landmark Press in the National Written & Illustrated By...Awards Contest for Students. Her deeply moving story, *Who Owns the Sun*, became part of the classroom library and a source of inspiration to my students.

Alexandra Wright of Newton, Massachusetts, began researching endangered species when she was in sixth grade. Her children's book, *Will We Miss Them? Endangered Species,* was published by Charlesbridge in 1992, followed by *At Home in the Tide Pool* (1993) and *Will You Be My Friend?* (1994).

Dozens of magazines and newspapers publish student writing. My own students have published their work in *Creative Kids Magazine, Young Writers Magazine*, and local newspapers. None of these students was what one might call a "gifted writer." Each had a story to tell and shared it in an interesting way. The possibility of publication motivated them to work through several drafts. Peter wrote about observing natural life in a state park. Stephanie wrote about meeting her father for the first time. Nick wrote about a deep-sea diving trip. Miriam wrote about immigrating from Russia. Bridgett won an essay contest related to a presidential campaign.

Do Your Homework

Do not keep the world of publication a secret from your students. If you are not familiar with the many opportunities for student publishing, then do your homework first. Read *The Market Guide for Young Writers* by Kathy Henderson (1988) for starters. This excellent book is packed with the how-tos of submission and detailed information on publication sources. Subscribe to a few magazines devoted to showcasing student writing such as *Creative Kids, Stone Soup*, and *Skipping Stones.*

The next step is to share this information with your class. Collect first-person articles from *Seventeen, American Girl*, and *Boys Life* for your students to read and model. Often, such articles prompt students to think about their own lives. What unique experiences have they had from which others could learn? Which issues are important to them?

Make a display of books and magazine articles written by young adults. Highlight famous authors who began writing when they were quite young, such as Louisa May Alcott, Lois Duncan, S. E. Hinton, Madeleine L'Engle, and Langston Hughes. Post notices of writing contests. Make a list of careers that uitilize writing talent. Invite book, magazine, and newspaper editors to speak to your class. Study the history of bookmaking and printing. Start an after-school writing club.

Encourage students who show interest and skill in writing by offering them opportunities to present their work to family and friends. Teach them how to polish their words until they shine. Then lead them to bigger challenges such as submitting work for publication.

SUCCESS STORY

Greg was a pleasant seventh-grader who went about his school work quietly and never made any trouble. He was one of those students who can easily be lost in the crowd. He had unusual interests, such as botany and entomology, and thus did not always fit into the mainstream of junior high school boys. Since I had several high-intensity and at-risk students in my class, I felt guilty that I too often left Greg (and others like him) waiting on the sideline.

One day, after a writing lesson on creating a setting, Greg handed in a paragraph that caught my attention. He vividly described his favorite spot at a national park in eastern Massachusetts. The details he focused on were unordinary, and thus made for a unique piece of writing. I wrote Greg a complimentary note and asked him if he would like to revise and expand the paragraph to submit for publication.

The next day, Greg was at my desk, his eyes bright and eager. After several revisions and conferences with me, Greg sent off his short essay to *Creative Kids Magazine*. Several weeks passed. One Friday evening, I received a phone call from Greg's father. He apologized for calling me at home, but Greg was dying to talk to me. Then he put his son on the line. "They're going to publish my essay!" Greg yelled. His father thanked me for taking the time to work with Greg. "This means a lot to him. He is really proud of himself. What a surprise to us!"

In school, I announced the good news and Greg passed around his acceptance letter. There were slaps on his back and high-fives. Greg blushed, but his face was beaming. Every student should have such a shining moment.

Perhaps you are thinking that there is little place in the language arts classroom for encouraging young people to attempt publication. Perhaps you think it is too unrealistic that they will meet with success, or you fear the effect of a rejected manuscript. Consider the wise analogy of Kathy Henderson (1988), author of *The Market Guide for Young Writers*.

I feel that young people are amazingly resilient. They are constantly seeking new challenges. Given an opportunity, they rebound. We witness this phenomenon each spring as Little Leaguers march up to the plate time and again ever hopeful of getting a meaningful hit. As adults, we consciously guard against letting them give up too quickly. Shouldn't this philosophy apply to young writers as well as young athletes? Not every Little Leaguer will succeed at the plate, and far fewer still will have Major League careers. Likewise, publishing success cannot be guaranteed for every writer. And only a handful of eager young writers will go on to careers in writing. But in the process, they will be learning valuable skills that will serve them in whatever future career they choose.

Meet a Young Author

My name is Cindy Peng. I'm twelve years old. Writing is an active part of me. I seem to do it naturally. My stories are about any subject I can think of, from flying horses to violin concerts. I enjoy having an open mind and use it often.

I especially enjoy writing poetry. My poetry has been published in *The Anthology of Poetry by Young Americans* and in a Chinese newspaper called *The World Journal.* I was also selected as one of the representatives from my school to attend the Rivier College Literacy Festival. I was the youngest student at the festival and won an Honorable Mention. I look forward to seeing the story I submitted, "The Silver Spur," published in a collection by Rivier College.

What probably helped me develop my writing skills the most was reading. I don't copy ideas from other books, but reading helps me expand my world and gives me new words to add to my vocabulary. I'm a book addict!

Now about my personal life. I live in Chelmsford, Massachusetts, with my mom, dad, and little brother Kevin, 2 rabbits, a turtle, a lot of fish, and 2 snails. I enjoy playing the violin and piano as well as playing soccer and computer games. My advice to beginning writers is: Dare to achieve your dreams. Shoot for the stars.

Sincerely,

Cindy Peng

Cindy Peng

Here is one of my poems that was featured in the *Kids Chronicle*, a newspaper published in Medford, MA.

MY BOOK AND I
By Cindy Peng

Amid the people in the library still,
There stands ME, with a quest to fulfill.
I search for a book, a treasure to find.
For I hunger for the excitement I could possess,
Just me and my mind.

I open book—now there's a brave venture!
For locked within is an enthralling adventure.
Hidden deep inside is a voyage to many places,
I travel to see and hear different creatures and faces.
With a book I can be a gnarled old wizard
or travel inside the gizzard of a lizard!

Books hold many stories to be told
I gasp in delight as the tales slowly unfold.

My book and I,
Together we can fly.

Book Talk

There are many words related to writing and publishing books that are useful to know.

1. Name an example of a book *trilogy*.

2. Where in a book might you find a *dedication?*

3. What information is found in a *book blurb?*

4. What is a book *sequel?*

5. Where in a book might you find an *epilogue?*

6. What is the purpose of a *preface?*

7. What does a book's *copyright* tell you?

8. Name a character in a book *series*.

9. What is the difference between a *novel* and a *novelization?*

10. What is an *anthology?*

11. Look on a book cover. Copy a line from a *reviewer's* comments.

References

Atwell, Nancie. (1987). *In the Middle: Writing, Reading, and Learning with Adolescents.* Portsmouth, NH: Boynton/Cook Heinemann, p. 106.

Bryan, Ashley. (1986). A tender bridge, in *Once Upon A Time....* New York: Putnam, p. 51.

Calkins, Lucy. (1986). *The Art of Teaching Writing.* Portsmouth, NH: Heinemann.

Henderson, Kathy. (1988). *Market Guide for Young Writers* (1988–89 ed.) Belvidere, NJ: Shoe Tree Press, p. xiii.

Hutchinson, Van. (1991, September). Vision and revision: Revising your writing. *Writing! 14*, No. 1.

Mazor, Harry. (1992). Big books, sex, and the classics: Some thoughts on teaching literature, in Donald Gallo (Ed.), *Author Insights.* Portsmouth, NH: Boynton/Cook, p. 6.

Murray, Donald. (1990). *Shoptalk: Learning to Write with Writers.* Portsmouth, NH: Boynton/Cook, p. 171.

Paterson, Katherine. (1981). *Gates of Excellence: On Reading and Writing for Children.* New York: Dutton.

Singer, Isaac Bashevis. (1990). In *Shoptalk: Learning to Write with Writers*, Donald M. Murray (Ed.), Portsmouth, NH: Heinemann.

Strunk, William Jr., & White, E. B. (1959). *The Elements of Style.* New York: Macmillan, p. ix.

Resources for Peer Editing

Christensen, Linda (Ed.). (1982). *A Guide to Teaching Self/Peer Editing.* Madison: University of Wisconsin.

Harp, Bill. (1988). Why aren't you using peer editing? *The Reading Teacher*, April: 828–830.

Authorship and Publishing

Asher, Sandy. (1989). *Wild Words! How to Train Them to Tell Stories.* Ill. by Denis Kendrick. New York: Walker.
Author of young adult stories Sandy Asher has written an engaging, easy-to-read guide for budding writers. Includes several examples from student writers. Good teacher resource for mini-lessons and writing exercises.

Bartlett, Susan. (1968). *Books: A Book to Begin On.* New York: Holt.
The development of bookmaking from early time to present, with emphasis on the milestones of progress.

Bauer, Marion Dane. (1992). *What's Your Story? A Young Person's Guide to Writing Fiction.* New York: Clarion.
A clear, practical guide that speaks to the budding writer. Grades 6–8.

Franklin, Jon. (1986). *Writing for Story. Craft Secrets of Dramatic Nonfiction by a Two-Time Pulitzer Prize Winner.* New York: Atheneum.
Especially good for talented young writers. Grades 8 and up.

Grant, Janet E. (1991). *Young Person's Guide to Becoming a Writer.* White Hall, VA: Shoe Tree Press.
This book offers excellent advice on developing characters, plot, setting, and writing in different genres. The information on submitting work for publication

is thorough and easy to follow. Though best suited for older teens, this book will appeal to talented and motivated younger students, and serve as a resource for creative writing teachers as well.

Greenfield, Howard. (1976). *Books: From Writer to Reader*. New York: Crown.
Each stage of a book's creation is explained. Grades 5 and up.

Hanson, Mary Lewis. (1979). *Your Career as a Writer*. New York: Arco.
Several career paths are explored for those who have good writing skills. Grades 5–9.

Hearn, Emily, & Thurman, Mark. (1990). *Draw & Write Your Own Picture Book*. Ontario: Pembroke Ltd.
A straightforward, easy-to-read guide to making picture books. The authors show children how to draw their stories first by using a story board before creating the words. Great for children who love drawing and have trouble putting ideas into words. Grades 4–7.

Henderson, Kathy. (1993). *Market Guide for Young Writers: Where and How to Sell What You Write* (4th ed.). Cincinnati, OH: Writer's Digest.
First published in 1986, this book offers sound advice for young writers ages eight to eighteen. Includes: extensive listings of places that accept work from young writers, contests and awards, profiles of editors and published young writers, and questions and answers on writing and publishing. Teachers can learn a lot from this book, too, especially regarding submission requirements and periodicals for young people. Inspiring and informative.

Judy, Susan, & Judy, Stephen. (1982). *Putting on a Play: A Guide to Writing and Producing Neighborhood Drama*. New York: Scribner. Grades 5–8.

King, Laurie, & Stovall, Dennis. (1992). *Classroom Publishing: A Practical Guide to Enhancing Student Literacy*. Hillsboro, OR: Blue Heron.
Everything you need to know about student publishing. Full of case studies, career information, resources, theory and practice, curricula, and testimonials.

Lewis, Amanda. (1992). *Writing: A Fact and Fun Book*. Ill. Heather Collins. Reading, MA: Addison-Wesley.
An engaging account of the history of writing from cave to computer, the development of writing tools, and book publishing. Includes instructions on calligraphy, bookbinding, and more. Grades 4–8.

McCaslin, Nellie. (1975). *Act Now! Plays and Ways to Make Them*. New York: S. G. Phillips.
Easy-to-follow advice for youngsters ages 10 to 14 on acting, writing, and producing plays, skits, and stories.

Melton, David. (1986). *Written & Illustrated by…*. Kansas City, MO: Landmark Editions.
This popular teacher's manual offers detailed instruction on all aspects of student publishing in the classroom. Contains lessons plans and illustrations. All grades.

Purdy, Susan. (1973). *Books for You to Make*. New York: Lippincott.
Writing and designing books is explored with main focus on binding materials and methods. Good teacher resource. Grades 5–8.

Schwartz, Alvin. (1981). *Scary Tales to Tell in the Dark*. New York: Lippincott.
Easy-to-read format of engaging tales. Good read-alouds.

Tchudi, Susan, & Tchudi, Stephen. (1984). *Young Writer's Handbook*. New York: Charles Scribner's Sons. Grades 5–8.
Suggests helpful procedures and approaches for beginning writers.

Weiss, Harvey. (1974). *How to Make Your Own Books*. New York: Crowell.
A children's guide to materials and procedures for making and decorating books. Grades 4–8.

Yates, Elizabeth. (1962). *Someday You'll Write*. New York: Dutton.
Advice to the young, aspiring writer. Grades 5–8.

You're the Author: From First Draft to Book. (1988). Pleasantville, NY: Sunburst Communications.
Illustrated activity cards provide step-by-step directions and hands-on experience in prewriting activities, writing, editing, proofreading, illustrating, and binding. Companion worksheets encourage creative thinking and reinforce basic skills. Activities are self-directed. Grades 4–6.

Characters as Writers

Byars, Betsy. (1988). *The Burning Question of Bingo Brown*. New York: Viking. Grades 4–6.

Cleary, Beverly. (1983). *Dear Mr. Henshaw*. New York: Morrow. Grades 3–6.

Colman, Hila. (1976). *Nobody Has to Be a Kid Forever*. New York: Pocket Books. Grades 4–6.

Elinovic, Zlata. (1994). *Zlata's Diary: A Child's Life in Sarajevo*. New York: Viking. Grades 6–9.

Fitzhugh, Louise. (1990). *Harriet the Spy*. New York: Harper and Row. Grades 4–6.

Gordam, Jane. (1971). *A Long Way from Verona*. New York: Macmillan. Grades 4–6.

Hahn, Mary Downing. (1983). *Daphne's Book*. New York: Clarion. Grades 5–7.

Hamm, D. J. (1990). *Bunkhouse Journal*. New York: Scribners. Grades 5–8.

Hassler, John. (1977). *Four Miles to Pinecone*. New York: Warne. Grades 7–9.

Hunter, Mollie. (1984). *Hold on to Love*. New York: Harper. Grades 7–10.

Montgomery, L. M. (1983). *Emily of New Moon*. New York: Bantam. Grades 6–9.

Montgomery, L. M. (1991). *Anne of Avonlea*. New York: Scholastic. Grades 5–9.

Naylor, Phyllis Reynolds. (1987). *Beetles, Lightly Toasted*. New York: Atheneum. Grades 4–6.

Sachs, Marilyn. (1979). *A Summer's Lease*. New York: Dutton. Grades 6–8.

Steele, Mary. (1991). Aunt Millicent, in T. Gascoigne, J. Goodman & M. Tyrell (Eds.), *Dream Time*. Boston: Houghton Mifflin. Grades 7–9.

Tolles, Martha. (1984). *Who's Reading Darci's Diary?* New York: Scholastic. Grades 4–6.

5

Discovering the Life
Behind the Words

I cannot remember a time when I did not consider myself a writer.
When I was three years old I was dictating stories to my parents, and
as soon as I learned to print, I was writing them down myself. I shared
a room with my younger brother, and at night I would lie in bed
inventing tales to give him nightmares.

—Lois Duncan (1985)

Children love to be let in on an author's "secrets." (Ray Bradbury, for instance, is afraid to fly in airplanes.) Every teenager I have taught was fascinated to know that S. E. Hinton wrote the, *The Outsiders* when she was only 16 years old. Working with elementary students in the Library Gang and junior high students in Reading Workshop convinced me that youngsters remember stories and poems when the writing is connected to the author's life. When my former students come back to visit, the first news I hear is what author they are studying in high school English. I remember Susannah telling me how proud she was to have been an expert on Edgar Allan Poe. "I knew things our teacher didn't!"

The "Amazing Authors" Curriculum

After a few years solely teaching Reading Workshop, I began teaching two sections of seventh- and eighth-grade English. The middle school program offers students thematic English courses for 12-week periods. Students select a course based on the catalogue description such as Mysteries, Heroes and Sheroes, and Three Novels. Naturally, I designed the Amazing Authors course (later changed to Famous Authors). Now I had a chance to test my author awareness approach with a larger and more heterogeneous group.

Although the initial curriculum design and gathering of materials was labor intensive, once done, I found the course easy to repeat. With each new class, I could refine and polish the curriculum. I never grew bored, as I could substitute literature selections, try a different activity, or study a new author.

During the years I worked on refining my author awareness approach, I gathered a wealth of information on authors. I clipped interviews and searched for biographies and books on the craft of writing. I saved book reviews and read hundreds of short stories and novels for young people.

Learning about authors and their creative processes is another way to help students develop author awareness. For many middle school students, the writing process is still an enigma. Why or how anyone becomes a writer is something a person may not even have considered. I use the following survey to stimulate thinking and discussion about writing and authors. Students' responses reveal their concepts of authorship.

1. How old must you be to publish your writing?
2. How long does it take to write a novel?
3. How do you become a writer? What talents do you need?
4. Who writes the stories in newspapers? Magazines? How does one go about getting a story published?
5. Why do writers write? How do writers write?

I assign question 5 as a composition on the first day of my Famous Authors course. This task baffles some students, yet other students already have a clear sense of what is involved in writing. This assignment helps me see the writing process through my students' eyes. Here are some student samples of this assignment.

WHY DO WRITERS WRITE?

Writers write because they enjoy writing and it gives them something to do. Instead of watching a movie on TV they sit at a comfortable place and start writing whatever comes to their mind.
Writers write because it's their job.
Usually writers write about something to get a message through to people or to say something about how he/she lived.

HOW DO WRITERS WRITE?
WHERE DO THEY GET IDEAS?

Writers write with a computer. Some use a pen.
Some writers outline; others brainstorm.
Writers get ideas from doing research.

After discussing these questions in class, I keep my students' answers. At the end of the course, I give the same assignment. I have always been pleased by the growth my students demonstrate in such a short time. Here are some excerpts from the second assignment.

WHY DO WRITERS WRITE?

Writers write about their feelings. For example, Langston Hughes writes about good and bad times growing up black. Robert Cormier's books are about reality of everyday life like drugs, crime, and murder.
Writers write because it is the thing they love most to do.
Writers write because they want to express themselves, share an experience with readers, or to make money in an enjoyable way.

HOW DO WRITERS WRITE?
WHERE DO THEY GET THEIR IDEAS?

Writers get their ideas from their imaginations, experiences, and observations.

Writers get ideas from many places. Paula Danziger gets ideas from interesting things that happened when she was a preteen. Langston Hughes writes about his experiences in Harlem.

Some writers research a topic or visit a place to see how people go about their everyday life. When Ray Bradbury writes a story about children, he might visit a playground.

Writing is hard, messy work. Writer's write by setting aside time, rehearsing, planning, revising, and editing.

There are many different ways to write. Nikki Giovanni gets inspired by reading and reading. She writes every day to get herself in the habit of recording her thoughts, feelings, and observations. Yoko Kawashima Watkins tries to make sense of her childhood war experiences by putting them into words. Isaac B. Singer writes in Yiddish and uses a translator. He is always changing his ideas and revising. On the other hand, Langston Hughes writes what comes to his mind in the form of poetry. He hardly ever changes his poems. He says they are "like rainbows. You have to catch them quickly before they disappear."

Help your students find out how and why their favorite authors write. *Speaking for Ourselves*, compiled and edited by Donald R. Gallo (1990), contains autobiographical sketches by notable authors of young adult books. My students laughed out loud as they read Paul Zindel's account of his frustrated English teacher. The kids noted that Zindel's life was very close to the characters in his books they had loved.

Before beginning a class novel, let students hear the voice of the author in these engaging autobiographical accounts. After reading several author sketches, students can work in groups to determine the characteristics writers share.

Another excellent source is *How Writers Write* by Pamela Lloyd (1987). Young adult authors talk about where their ideas come from, how and where they write, and the revision and publishing process. I have my students compare work habits of writers. Then I ask how the habits of professional writers differ from their own way of composing.

Writer and teacher Donald Murray (1990) has compiled a treasury of quotations from writers in *Shoptalk: Learning to Write with Writers*. Murray thinks that students gain confidence in their writing when they discover that they, too, share the struggles, feelings, and experience of published writers.

> *School often teaches unnatural, "nonwriterly" attitudes toward writing—know what you want to say before you say it.... Published writers do not write under the kind of research conditions inexperienced writers can be placed under in the classroom.... Often these conditions and the assignments are inappropriate if you know what writers do and how they do it.*

I prompt students to think about their own writing methods by using the following questions:

- What is the hardest part about writing for you? What is the easiest part?
- What steps do you take when you write a story? How about when you write an essay?
- What kinds of writing do you like? Not like?
- Where do you get your ideas? What experience in your life could you write about?
- What knowledge could you share with others through writing?
- What do you do when the writing is not going well?

Awareness of the Writing Process

With the advent of the whole language movement, great emphasis has been placed on teaching writing as a process. While this approach has been widely accepted for its good results, we must be careful not to impose a single process on every student. One process that is commonly taught involves five steps: brainstorming, first draft, revision, final draft, and publication.

Students should learn and try out this process, but they should also be exposed to other alternatives. It is unfair to insist that all students use the same process for all writing. Some writing will require several drafts. Some writers start with the ending. Others use a tape recorder for their first drafts. Teachers should help students learn different processes and discover which one work best for them.

One way to develop students' awareness of their own processes is to have students attach to a writing assignment a prepared form that briefly describes the process they used. The form can include where the idea came from, any problems encountered, the number of drafts written, where and when the writing took place, students' feelings about the piece, and help received.

Discovering the life behind the words, exploring the author's methods, and focusing on their own methods gets students thinking about writing in a broader sense—as something more than just a school assignment. Students learn what real writers do, how writing is used in the real world, and the various ways to approach a writing task. Finally, we must give our students the tools to write well while they discover their own way of using them.

Author Study

In designing my Famous Authors course, I presented writers of different genres, enthnicities, eras, and styles. I also wanted authors whose lives and works are interesting and accessible to middle school students. I remember being forced to read *Silas Marner* in the eighth grade. Considering how many engaging classics exist, I cannot understand why my teacher (or the administration) chose this book (not to mention the dull way in which it was presented).

As the teacher of Famous Authors, I did not select authors because I thought they were "good" for my students. You will notice that Shakespeare is missing from my course list. I did not feel I could do justice to this master, given the time constraint of the course. Our school was fortunate to have an excellent teacher who offered a 13-week course on Shakespeare and one of his plays.

Another criterion for selecting authors is that I enjoy their works as well as know something about their lives. A teacher with a passion for an author such as Thoreau can often pique the interest of even the most jaded adolescent. Think back to the authors that inspired and entertained you. Reread their works. Research their lives. And don't be afraid to learn alongside your students.

I think it is important to give children a sense of the time in which an author lived. I always begin by asking the class what they know about the events and lifestyle of a particular period. When was television invented? The lightbulb? How did people travel? What style of clothes was popular? Who was the U.S. president? What other authors wrote during this time? Studying an author's life integrates well with history.

Pictures are important, too. Whenever possible, show kids the face of an author. The author's speaking voice adds another dimension as well. I have found recordings of Langston Hughes and Robert Frost reading their poetry, and Roald Dahl reading his novels. A Public Television documentary on Isaac Bashevis Singer allowed students to hear the author's thick Yiddish accent as well to see the author at the Nobel Prize ceremony.

The following guide is to help you create your own author study units. Whether you spend three days or three weeks on an author is up to you. The suggested authors, literature selections, and activities were all classroom tested at the seventh- and eighth-grade levels, yet are easily adapted for younger students.

Emily Dickinson

There is no Frigate like a book to take us Lands away.

The mysteries of Dickinson's curious life appeal to young readers. Why did she never marry? Why did she not leave her home for so many years? Why was she taken to wearing white dresses? Why was she not published during her lifetime?

Of her 1775 recorded poems, there are dozens that are accessible to children, as Dickinson herself often assumed the persona of a child. I like to present her poems as an "old-fashioned mystery" and encourage my students to free associate and hunt for the meaning behind her metaphors.

Dickinson was a passionate letter writer and nature lover. As a young girl, she read voraciously and was greatly influenced by such greats as the Bible, hymns, Shakespeare, Emerson, the Brontë sisters, and Elizabeth Browning.

BIOGRAPHY

1. What life was like in nineteenth-century Amherst, Massachusetts
2. Emily's early education and religious life
3. Family influences and relationships
4. Eccentricities and seclusion in midlife

Dickinson's poems are mostly untitled. I have used key words from the first lines to identify the poem.

POETRY

1. Nobody
2. Letter to the World
3. If I can stop one heart
4. No frigate like a book
5. A word is dead
6. Hope is the thing with feathers
7. Will there really be a morning?
8. A soft sea washed around
9. I never saw moor
10. In this short life

ACTIVITIES

1. Draw images. What themes and subjects are expressed?
2. Identify "special effects" (unusual words, mixed-up grammar, distinct meter, interesting word combinations).
3. Memorize a favorite poem.
4. Write a short biography of Dickinson's life. Use her poetry to illustrate the events, people, places, and concerns of her life.
5. Read the letters of Emily Dickinson. Select several quotes that describe life in nineteenth-century New England.
6. Read the poetry of Walt Whitman; compare and contrast to Dickinson's work.

RESOURCES

Bedard, Michael. (1992). *Emily*. New York: Doubleday.
    This exquisite 32-page children's book tells of a brief encounter between a young girl and her strange neighbor—Emily Dickinson. The text itself is rich with imagery, and Barbara Cooney's beautiful oil paintings reflect nineteenth-century New England life. Michael Bedard researched Emily's life and visited the Dickinson homestead before writing this story.

Bolin, Frances Schoonmaker (Ed.). (1994). *Poetry for Young People: Emily Dickinson*. New York: Sterling.

Emily Dickinson: American Poet. (1995, March). *Cobblestone*. Entire issue.

Emily Dickinson: 75 Poems and Letters, audiocassette. Recorded Books, Inc. 1-800-638-1304.

Greene, Carol. (1990). *Emily Dickinson: American Poet*. Chicago: Children's Press.

Luce, William. (1976). *The Belle of Amherst*. Boston: Houghton Mifflin. A one-woman play that incorporates quotes from Dickinson's letters and poems.

Olsen, Victoria. (1990). *Emily Dickinson*. New York: Chelsea.

Sewall, Richard B. (1974). *The Life of Emily Dickinson*. New York: Farrar.

Langston Hughes

Poems are like rainbows: they escape you quickly.

There are numerous books written on this wonderful man's life, including his auto-biography. Hughes was one of the first black writers to write for other blacks in their voice. Though known primarily as a poet, he also wrote operas, gospel music, plays, novels, essays, short stories, black history books, and humorous articles. His poetry is easy to read and has a lyrical quality.

BIOGRAPHY

1. Read aloud excerpts from *The Big Sea* and Milton Meltzer's biography (see Resources).

DISCUSSION

1. How did books help Langston during his childhood?
2. How might Langston's grandmother have influenced his future as a writer?
3. Why do you suppose Langston said that "some of my best poems were written when I felt the worst"?
4. What was life like in Harlem in 1924?

The first four poems are short and simple with beautiful imagery. The last poem is a bit longer and more complex.

POETRY

1. "Dreams"
2. "Dream Keeper"
3. "Border Line"
4. "My People"
5. "April Rain Song"

6. "The Songs on Seventh Street"
7. "Border Line"
8. "The Negro Speaks of Rivers"

ACTIVITIES

1. Read each poem aloud several times. Look at the physical construction of the poem. Look for patterns.
2. Use symbols to illustrate the themes in each poem.
3. Write about your own dreams.
4. Identify on a map the geographical references in "The Negro Speaks of Rivers."

For additional study of Langston's poetry, encourage students to look for biographical poems, poems based on his travels to Africa and Mexico, and racial poems.

SHORT STORIES

1. "Thank you M'am"   A young boy attempts to steal a woman's purse and is taken by surprise when she has the last word. This story is very short and kids find the plot and element of surprise interesting. Its tight construction and strong characterization make it an excellent model of short story writing. I like to reread the first paragraph aloud to demonstrate how much information Langston Hughes jam-packed into the opening.
   a. Working in pairs, have students write a list of information that can be inferred from the story.
   b. Write a journal entry the boy might have written after his encounter with Mrs. Jones.

RESOURCES

Berry, S. L. (1993). *Langston Hughes*. Mankato, MN: Creative Education.

Cooper, Floyd. (1994). *Coming Home: From the Life of Langston Hughes*. New York: Philomel.

Haskins, James S. (1976). *Always Movin' On: The Life of Langston Hughes*. New York: Watts.

Hughes, Langston. (1940). *The Big Sea*. New York: Knopf.

Larson, Norita D. (1981). *Langston Hughes, Poet of Harlem*. Mankato, MN: Creative Education.

Meltzer, Milton. (1968). *Langston Hughes: A Biography*. New York: Crown.

Poetry and Reflections. (1980). Performed by Hughes on audiocassette. Harper-Caedmon.

Rampersad, Arnold, & Roessel, David. (Eds.). (1996). *The Collected Poems of Langston Hughes*. New York: Vintage Classics.

Maya Angelou

Life doesn't frighten me at all.

Poet, writer, singer, dancer, teacher, editor, playwright, speaker, and songwriter are among the many descriptions of this amazing woman's career. She was the first black woman to write a screenplay for a movie, and the first to direct one. This is a writer who has truly lived! Her poetry and autobiographical books reflect the pain, trauma, and survival of her childhood as well as her strength, hope, and joy. At the inauguration of President Clinton in 1993, Angelou read a poem she had written for that occasion. Maya Angelou has risen to achieve international literary fame.

BIOGRAPHY

1. Excerpts from her autobiography, *I Know Why the Caged Bird Sings*; View film (most suitable for grades 7 and 8)
2. Library research on biographical data and author interviews
3. Compare life to Langston Hughes

POETRY

1. "And Still I Rise" (a powerful, famous poem; the seventh stanza describes a sexual image)
2. "Life doesn't frighten me"
3. "On Aging"
4. "Harlem Hopscotch"
5. "On the Pulse of Morning"

ACTIVITIES

1. Do a choral reading of the poetry.
2. Explore rhythms and patterns of poems.
3. What emotions are expressed? Which lines do you like?
4. Compare the poetry of Maya Angelou and Langston Hughes.

RESOURCES

Elliot, Jeffrey M. (Ed.). (1988). *Conversations with Maya Angelou.* University, MS: University Press of Mississippi.

Kallen, Stuart A. (1993). *Maya Angelou: Woman of Words, Deeds and Dreams.* Kansas City, MO: Abdo.

BOOKS BY MAYA ANGELOU

I Know Why The Caged Bird Sings (Random House, 1970)
Oh Pray My Wings Are Gonna Fit Me Well (Random House, 1974)
And Still I Rise (Random House, 1978)
Shaker Why Don't You Sing (Random House, 1983)
All God's Children Need Travelin' Shoes (Random House, 1986)
On the Pulse of Morning (Random House, 1993)

Isaac Bashevis Singer

*When I was a child they called me a liar; when I was an adult they
called me a writer.*

Singer's stories, mostly translated from Yiddish, are treasures to read aloud. These fairy-folktale-like stories are deeply rooted in the culture of nineteenth-century Poland. Rich in humor, fantasy, and meaning, Singer's tales explore universal themes such as wisdom, survival, faith, and love. Singer believes that children of all ages are deeply concerned with the questions people have asked since the beginning of time.

Enter in to his forgotten world of blacksmiths and butchers, demons and angels, and wise rabbis and curious children.

BIOGRAPHY

1. Life in a turn-of-the-century Polish village and culture of that time
2. Isaac Singer as a young boy
3. Literary accomplishments

SHORT STORIES

1. "Utzel and his Daughter Poverty"   This is a timeless fable about a lazy man who wants to be rich without working.
   a. Read aloud and stop before the last line. Have the students guess the motto: "Whatever you can do today, don't put off till tomorrow."
   b. In what ways do you procrastinate? Has it ever brought you trouble?
2. "The Power of Light"   Two children flee to freedom during World War II.
   a. Before reading, explore associations with the word *light*. What is the holiday Hanukkah?
   b. After reading, explore themes of survival, inner strength, and faith.
3. "Zlateh the Goat"   With the help of the family goat, young Aaron survives getting lost in a snowstorm during Hanukkah.
   a. Compare plot and theme to "Power of Light."
   b. How does Singer paint a picture of the snowstorm?
4. "Naftali the Storyteller and His Horse Sus"   Naftali, who loves stories so much, grows up to devote his life to spreading stories throughout. Those who don't tell stories and don't hear stories live only for that moment, and that isn't enough. This story, for experienced listeners, deserves a second reading.
   a. Find references to the setting and era.
   b. Study the advice and wisdom of Reb Falik. What do his words mean? Do you agree with them?
   c. Why are stories so important to us? Look at examples for history, such as Greeks, Native Americans, Africans, and so on.

RESOURCES

Kresh, Paul. (1984). *Isaac Bashevis Singer: Story of a Storyteller.* New York: Dutton.

The Power of Light: Eight Stories for Hannukah. (1980). New York: Farrar.

Stories for Children: Isaac Bashevis Singer. (1984). New York: Farrar.

O. HENRY

Most autobiographies are insincere from beginning to end, and about the only chance for truth to be told is in fiction.

William Syndey Porter, alias O. Henry, wrote hundreds of short stories during the late 1800s. He is best known for his surprise endings. My students have enjoyed his engaging plots, although he can be overly detailed at times and some of the language in his short stories may be unfamiliar and outdated. The abridged versions of his stories work quite well.

BIOGRAPHY

1. Prepare a time line of his life.

SHORT STORIES

1. "Gift of the Magi"   This classic Christmas tale about the true meaning of gift giving has been adapted and retold in film, print, and on the stage.
   a. Rewrite an updated version of the story.
   b. Write about a very special gift you received.
   c. Act out the story.
2. "One Thousand Dollars"   A young man inherits $1,000 from his uncle and solicits advice as to how to spend the money.
   a. Write about what you would do with $1,000.
   b. Identify the twists in the short story.
   c. Rewrite the story as a play.
3. "The Last Leaf"   An aspiring young artist loses the will to live and is helped along by an elderly neighbor.
   a. Identify the twists in the story.
   b. Explore themes of hope and sacrifice.

AUTHOR AWARENESS

1. Find parallels in O. Henry's life and his stories.
2. Identify similarities among the three stories.
3. Discuss the meaning of irony and how O. Henry makes use of this device.
4. Draw a scene from each story. Select a direct quote as the caption.

EXTENSION ACTIVITY

1. Write a short story with a twist or surprise ending.

RESOURCES

The Best of O. Henry. (1978). Philadelphia: Running Press.

The Best Short Stories of O. Henry. (1948). New York: Modern Library.

The Gift of the Magi. (1972). Ill. by Erik Blegvad. New York: Hawthorn.

The Gift of the Magi. (1980). Ill. by Byron Glasser. Mankato, MN: Creative Education.

Long, E. Hudson. (1960). *O. Henry: The Man and His Work.* New York: Barnes.

The World of O. Henry, audiocassette. Recorded Books, Inc. 1-800-638-1304.

Edgar Allan Poe

All that we see or seem is but a dream within a dream.

"Long before Stephen King, there was Mr. Poe—the true Father of Gore." This is how I introduce the man believed to have written the first detective story. "Imagine a time before television, radio, and Hollywood horror movies. The story you're about to hear is over 150 years old. People still read it, feel its terror, and study its special effects. We know "The Tell-Tale Heart" is a masterpiece because it has survived this long. That is what makes a classic story. Poe died tragically in 1849. His life alone is a fascinating tale."

BIOGRAPHY

1. Assign each student a question on Poe's life; allow a few days to research answers. In class, combine the clues to his tragic and mysterious life.

SHORT STORIES

1. "The Tell-Tale Heart"   I give a lot of time to this story. I want all students to understand the plot as well as appreciate its craftsmanship. This is a high-interest story that can be read on multiple levels, making it an ideal selection for a heterogeneous class. Students really want to hear it a few times and enjoy the delicious description such as, "One of his eyes resembled that of a vulture…a dull blue with a hideous veil over it."

Providing opportunities to stretch their minds through the the close study of classic literature gives students a sense of mastery and builds confidence in reading. You must know the material beforehand, though. Then entice and engage your students as you guide them through Poe's work.

STRATEGIES

1. It is essential that students hear the story of "The Tell-Tale Heart" first, preferably on an an audio cassette by a professional reader. (One with sound effects makes it even better.) Then have students reconstruct the events. This gives you an idea of how much they absorbed just by listening.
2. Next, I give the students copies of the story and a vocabulary list complete with definitions. Though the vocabulary is difficult, much can be gleaned through context: "I know you'll love this strange tale, but let's look at the meaning of some difficult words Poe uses." I do not care for the abridged versions. I want my students to hear the richness of Poe's language that creates the mood and strong imagery.
3. Read the words aloud. Which words do they recognize? Which words sound interesting? Who can find another meaning for "dead body"? Discuss the meanings. Then students might complete a vocabulary worksheet, crossword puzzle, or hunt for the words in context.
4. Next, students read along while again listening to the tape (or the teacher reading aloud), which aides comprehension. Students are using visual and auditory modes. The new vocabulary is also reinforced. Since the story is a confession, hearing it told with precision and passion heightens the dramatic effect.
5. Students work in pairs answering author awareness questions. Other activities include simile and metaphor hunt; creating a story time line; identifying setting, conflict, and mood; discussing point of view; and cloze exercises (fill in vocabulary words in context).
6. Students find a favorite passage of at least 25 words and copy the passage onto an index card. Challenge them to memorize the quote with the option of reciting it for the class or writing it down from memory.
7. I read the story once more in class, this time giving students a chance to read aloud. We look for special effects and discuss the structure of the story. Students who had trouble understanding the story may now say, "Aha!"; others may uncover deeper meanings. Difficult passages become clearer.

POETRY

1. "Annabelee"
2. "The Raven"
3. "The Bells"

These famous poems are wonderful to hear. Again, a professional recording is best. Let your students feel the rhythm and flow of these classic poems without overanalyzing them.

RESOURCES

Basil Rathbone reads Edgar Allan Poe. Caedmon, 1964.

The Best of Edgar Allan Poe. Listening Library, 1980.

Edgar Allan Poe Foundation, Inc. 1914 E. Main St. Richmond, VA 23223.

Ghostly Tales and Eerie Poems of Edgar Allan Poe. (1993). Ill. by Larry Schwinger. New York: Grosset and Dunlap.

Poe, Edgar Allan. (1980). *The Tell-Tale Heart.* Ill. by Byron Glasser. Mankato, MN: Creative Education.

S. E. Hinton

I advise writing to oneself. If you don't want to read it, nobody else is going to read it.

S. E. Hinton's classic young adult book, *The Outsiders*, was published in 1967, when the author was age 16. Her books have appealed to youngsters for their universal conflicts, compelling characters, and gritty realism. She is one of the few authors that I wait to introduce after students have read the book. In fact, I try not to reveal that she is female. This makes for an interesting discussion on point of view (*The Outsiders* has a male viewpoint) and writing talent.

In my Famous Authors course, S. E. Hinton was among the 10 authors we studied. Although we did not have time to read her novels as a class, I found that reading excerpts of her work motivated the children to seek out the books on their own. Also, the first chapter of *The Outsiders* works well on its own, especially as an example of character description.

NOVELS

1. *The Outsiders*
   a. Find an original book review of *The Outsiders*. What main points does the reviewer make? Do you agree?
   b. Make a "Wanted" poster for one of the characters.
   c. Compare the movie to the book.
   d. Write a poem that captures the essence of the book.

DISCUSSION

1. What special effects does Hinton use? How does she bring her characters to life? Which character would you like to meet and why?
2. Identify the types of conflict in the book.
3. *The Outsiders* was first published in 1967. In what ways are the themes, characters, and plot still relevant today? How might the novel differ if it were written by a teenager today?

RESOURCES

Daly, Jay. (1987). *Presenting S. E. Hinton.* Boston: Twayne.

Hinton S. E. (1967). *The Outsiders.* New York: Dell.

Paul Zindel

*I think action and suspense are the most important elements in all of
writing for young people.*

Paul Zindel was a high school chemistry teacher for seven years before writing his Pulitzer Prize–winning play, *The Effect of Gamma Rays on Man-in-the-Moon Marigolds*. His first novel, *The Pigman*, published in 1968, began the evolution of the genre called adolescent literature.

Zindel's zany novels parallel his own youth. I find that looking at Zindel's life after reading his works has a greater impact on the students. They can see how a person's early life often shapes his or her work as an author.

I had the pleasure of meeting Paul Zindel at an International Reading Association Conference. He was as funny and engaging a speaker as he is a writer. My students were delighted when I returned from the convention with more anecdotes from their favorite author's life, as well as an autographed copy of his new book, *The Amazing and Death-Defying Diary of Eugene Dingman*.

RESOURCES

Forman, Jack J. (1988). *Presenting Paul Zindel*. Boston: Twayne.

Hipple, Theodore W. (1988). *A Teacher's Guide to the Novels of Paul Zindel*. New York: Bantam Books.
   An informative 40-page booklet available from Bantam Doubleday Dell, 666 Fifth Avenue, New York, NY 10103.

Zindel, Paul. (1968). *The Pigman*. New York: Harper and Row.

Zindel, Paul. (1977). *Confessions of a Teenage Baboon*. New York: Harper and Row.

Zindel, Paul. (1991). *The Pigman & Me*. New York: Bantam.
   A hilarious account of the most important year in Zindel's teenage life. Meet the inspiration for *The Pigman* and other book characters. Zindel speaks directly to children on their level; he'll crack you up, too.

Ray Bradbury

I don't need an alarm clock. My ideas wake me up.

Many of Ray Bradbury's short stories are highly appealing to middle school students. His stories have more the feeling of Twilight Zone than pure science fiction. They spark and stretch the imagination. His characters, many of them children, are very human. Read about an illustrated man with tattoos that tell stories, a Martian colony, a boy who stays 12 years old forever, and a school field trip into the past. Ray Bradbury's is a master of metaphor and description, and thus is an excellent model for vivid writing.

SHORT STORIES

1. "All Summer in a Day"   A lonely young girl living in a space colony on Venus awaits the arrival of the sun, which appears once every seven years.
   a. Read silently then aloud in class.
   b. Look for figurative language.
   c. Discuss ambiguous ending. Write a continuation.
   d. What is science fiction? What facts and fiction are in this story?

2. "Fever Dream"   A bedridden boy experiences strange sensations during a serious illness.
    a. Before reading: Recall a time you were very sick. What happens to your body and mind when you have a high fever?
    b. After reading: What do you think really happened in the story? What does the ending mean? What clues did the author give?
    c. Look for examples of figurative language that creates a vivid mental picture.
    d. How would you translate the story into a film?

RESOURCES

Bradbury, Ray. (1951). *The Illustrated Man.* New York: Doubleday.

Bradbury, Ray. (1972). *The Halloween Tree.* Ill. by Joe Mugnaini. New York: Random House.

Bradbury, Ray. (1976). *Long After Midnight.* New York: Knopf.

Ray Bradbury Reads 19 Complete Stories, audiocassette Audio Partners, 1985.

Strange Tales: Ray Bradbury, videorecording by Atlantis Films. (Thorn EMI/HBO, 1986.

The Veldt, videorecording by Atlantis Films. Beacon Films, 1989.

Author	Birthdate/Place	Background Info	Genres/Themes	Special Effects

Titles of Works		Awards/Interesting Facts		Quotes from the Author	

Story	Author	Setting/Mood	Characters	Conflict	Theme

Group Activities for Author Study

Find Your Match

This is a fun introduction to a unit on authors. On an index card, write the name of a famous author. Write the title of a famous work by that author on another index card. Do the same for several authors. Make enough cards for your class. Distribute one card to each student. Ask the students how quickly they can find their matches. Afterwards, the youngsters introduce themselves and ask the class to decide whether or not the match is correct. You can also play this game with authors and their famous characters.

To Tell the Truth

Here is a fun way to practice careful reading and review an author study. Have students carefully read an author biographical sketch in class or for homework. Demonstrate note taking and underlining strategies beforehand. Select three students to be on the panel. Each panel member pretends to be the featured author, but only one will tell the truth. Class members take turns asking the panel questions about the "author's" life and works. (All answers must be contained in the biographical sketch.) The class has to determine which panel member is telling the truth. You can set a time or question limit. To make the game more difficult, have students play without their notes.

Literary Map

In small groups, students create maps of the United States and other continents. After researching the birthplaces of famous authors around the world, students label the country, city, or state with the author's name and literary work.

Amazing Author Facts

This library activity develops research skills. Using several reference books, students skim the author biographies for unusual and interesting facts about the writer's life. Encourage students to look for facts that others will find enlightening, amusing, or amazing. Later, all facts are compiled and the list is copied for the class.

Who Am I?

Assign students to prepare "Who am I?" statements on the authors they have studied. In small groups, have the students quiz each other. (Example: My first published story was "The Golden Bug." Who am I? Answer: Edgar Allan Poe.) Another version is to have a student (or yourself) represent a secret author. The class tries to guess the author's identity by asking yes or no questions. If they cannot guess the identity in 10 questions, then the "author" wins.

Author Jeopardy

This activity is always a hit. Students are motivated to practice study skills and work cooperatively. I give the class a couple days' notice before Jeopardy Day. I also provide class time for students to work together in reviewing the authors and the literature.

The game is played similarly to the television show. Possible categories are Who Am I?, Short Stories, Who Wrote It?, Specific Authors, Special Effects, Birthplaces, Memorable Characters, Author Quotes, and so on. Prepare the Jeopardy grid on a sheet of paper. This will be your game key. Fill in each box with an answer to which a student will supply the question. Answers should increase in difficulty as you go down the column.

To play, draw a large 5×5 grid on the board or on an overhead projector (see Figure 5–1). Divide class into two teams seated on opposite sides of the board. The first player on Team A selects a category and point value. For example, "I'll take Scott

FIGURE 5–1 Jeopardy Grid

O'Dell	Alcott	Poe	Cleary	Twain
5	5	5	5	5
10	10	10	10	10
15	15	15	15	15
20	20	20	20	20
25	25	25	25	25

O'Dell for 15." The teacher reads the corresponding answer on the grid: "This book was based on a diary." The student has 10 seconds to supply the question ("What is *Island of the Blue Dolphin*"?).

Record 15 points on the board under Team A. If the student's question is incorrect, the corresponding person on Team B gets a chance to supply the correct question to the same answer. If Team B cannot supply the correct question, neither team receives the 15 points and the teacher supplies the answer. If either team gives an incorrect response, then the points are deducted from the team score.

To continue, cross out the number 15 under Scott O'Dell. Team B continues with the next player. When Team A is up again, the second player takes the turn. When all the categories have been used, the team with the highest score wins.

With very small teams, you can play more closely to the television show by using hand raising or bell ringing to indicate a student knows the question. Daily doubles and bonus questions are fun, too. *Warning*: This version is exciting but can get out of hand!

Author Scavenger Hunt

Prepare a list of interesting items for students to find by using the libary or computer database to find the answers (see samples, page 119). I have given students a week to complete the hunt and offered extra credit or prizes to the first correct entry. You might ask students to supply the source as well.

Individual and Partner Projects for Author Study

There is simply not enough time to introduce all the authors I would like. To get around this problem, I assign students to become an expert on one famous author. Students may work individually or with a partner. The final project is presented to the class. This is a fun way of "meeting" many more authors. I prepare a list of author choices, usually writers we have not studied in class. After reviewing the list, students decide whether they want to work alone or with a partner. As choices are made, I jot down the student's name next to the author. Here are some suggestions:

FAMOUS AUTHORS OF YESTERYEAR

Hans Christian Anderson	C. S. Lewis
Frank Baum	Jack London
Emily Brontë	A. A. Milne
Lewis Carroll	Lucy Maude Montgomery

Agatha Christie	Edgar Allan Poe
Beverly Cleary	Beatrix Potter
Roald Dahl	William Shakespeare
Charles Dickens	Murasaki Shikibu
Emily Dickinson	Robert Louis Stevenson
Frederick Douglass	Harriet Beecher Stowe
Sir Arthur Conan Doyle	J. R. R. Tolkien
Robert Frost	Mark Twain (Samuel Clemens)
Theodor Geisel (Dr. Seuss)	E. B. White
Langston Hughes	Laura Ingalls Wilder
Rudyard Kipling	

I have had great success with the author expert project. Here are some tips for smooth sailing:

- Save samples of projects so students have a model.
- Show students how to locate information on the author. Introduce the various reference sources. Our school librarian gave a mini-lesson to my class.
- Break down the research process into steps: locating sources, reading, note taking.
- Before they begin researching, ask students to write down what they want to know about the author.
- For inexperienced researchers and students with learning disabilities, make a note-taking sheet with labeled categories.
- Model and teach note-taking techniques. Monitor student progress.

Author Expert Research Choices

Author Interview

Write an interview with the author that could appear in a magazine or newspaper article. Use the Question/Answer format. *Hint:* Give some time and thought to the questions. Don't just ask, "When were you born?" A better question would be: "Tell me about where you grew up." Your questions and the author's answers should sound *natural.* Also, the author should say much more than the interviewer!

TV Talk Show

With a partner, stage a mock television interview. Make it lively and interesting. Have copies of the author's books on hand. Make sure to discuss the writer's work as well as her or his life. *Hint:* Try writing a script first. Make the dialogue sound natural. You may perform for the class or videotape the interview. Be sure to practice.

Children's Biography

Write an author's biography geared for children ages 7 to 10. Illustrate the text or cut out pictures. Make a sturdy cover. *Hint:* Think about what a young reader would want to know. Focus on the personal and interesting parts of the author's life. Aim for a simple and engaging writing style. (Study examples of published biographies.)

Time Line

Create a detailed, illustrated time line of the author's life and published works. *Hint:* Try using one 8 × 11½ sheet of paper for each date. Tape the papers together to make the finished time line.

Author Expert Project Pointers

1. Decide on your method of presentation.

2. Make a list of questions and areas of interest.

3. Find at least two references, such as:
   a. Newspaper/magazine articles
   b. Interviews
   c. Book reviews
   d. Obituaries
   e. Autobiographies/biographies
   f. Biographical sketches
   g. Letters/photographs
   h. Data bases

4. Read for answers to your questions, as well as for additional information and background information. Take notes.

5. Read selections of the author's work. This should be at least one of the following: a novel, four short stories, one play, or 20 poems. Note subjects, themes, and characters. Look for parallels between the author's life and work.

6. Organize your notes into categories such as early years. Then decide if you have enough information.

7. Use your research to complete the presentation.

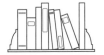

Author Expert Research Form

EARLY YEARS   *IMPORTANT INFLUENCES*

EDUCATION   *JOBS/CAREER*

FAMOUS WRITINGS   *GENRES/THEMES/STYLES*

AUTHOR'S PERSONALITY/WRITING HABITS

Characters and Their Creators

Our imaginations have the power to create characters. Here are some favorite characters that famous writers have brought to life. See if you can match the character to its creator.

1. Lassie _____

2. Snoopy _____

3. Frankenstein _____

4. Romeo _____

5. Alice in Wonderland _____

6. Wilbur the Pig _____

7. Homer Price _____

8. Nancy Drew _____

9. Dorothy and Toto _____

10. The Cat-in-the-Hat _____

11. Sherlock Holmes _____

12. Inspector H. Poirot _____

13. Heidi _____

14. Peter Rabbit _____

15. Bilbo _____

L. Frank Baum	Lewis Carroll	William Shakespeare
J. R. R. Tolkien	Robert McCloskey	E. B. White
Charles Schulz	Agatha Christie	Johanna Spyri
Mary Shelley	Dr. Seuss	Sir Arthur Conan Doyle
Eric Knight	Beatrix Potter	Carolyn Keene

Author Search

Use a author reference book to complete the following questions.

1. Where did E. B. White grow up? _____
From where did he get his inspiration for his book *Charlotte's Web?*

_____

What awards did he receive? _____

_____

2. What type of books did Jack London write? _____

_____

What life experiences do you think most influenced Jack London's

writing? Why? _____

_____

_____

3. Which beloved children's author wrote under the pen name of The-

odor Geisel? _____

List an interesting fact about this man.

_____

4. Copy a quote from Katherine Paterson that reveals her thoughts on
writing for young people.

_____

_____

_____

5. What famous fictional character did Sir Arthur Conan Doyle create?

_____

What influence or inspiration may have led Conan Doyle to create

this character? _____

6. What was unusual about Hans Christian Anderson's education?

_____

7. What genre is Agatha Christie best known for?

_____

Which book is considered to be one of her most difficult to solve?

_____

8. Which famous story did Frank Baum create? _____

_____

Have you ever read this book?_____

What question would you like to ask him? _____

_____

9. List three interesting facts about the poet Myra Cohn Livingston.

_____

_____

_____

Copy a few lines of a poem you like.

_____

_____

10. Name three books by Arnold Lobel.

_____

_____

_____

What other talent does he have?

_____

_____

Children's Literature Scavenger Hunt

Can you find....?

1. An author/illustrator? _____

_____

2. A book published by Random House? _____

_____

3. A book of poetry? _____

_____

4. An alphabet book? _____

_____

5. A book by Ashley Bryan? _____

_____

6. A book by Dr. Seuss published in 1978? _____

_____

7. A book with one of your classmate's names in the title? _____

_____

8. The author of *Winnie-the-Pooh?* _____

_____

9. An author who retells Cinderella? _____

_____

10. A book that takes place in the country? _____

_____

More Classroom Activities
for Author Awareness

Author Puzzles

Provide a variety of puzzles for the students: word searches, crosswords, scrambled words, matching, and so on. Students can also make their own for classmates.

Author Categories

Create a card game by writing the name of a different author on several index cards. Students divide the cards into mystery writers, author/illustrators, science fiction, humor, and poetry. Provide an answer sheet or reference book for self-checking.

Author Trivia

Give the students questions cards, a standard game board, four playing pieces, and a rule sheet. They ask each other the author questions and move according to the rules.

Author Detective

Students complete a Missing Author Report by using information given in popular trade books, author biographies, computer software, or other reference sources.

Author Expert

Give a certificate, badge, or token to those students who complete several of the above activities.

Happy Birthday, Dear Author

Honor an author's birthday each month. Challenge the students to find the author's books and background information. Display the writer's books.

Amazing Authors

Enlist your students' help in creating a bulletin board of photos of famous authors. Think of different ways to group writers, such as: Authors for Our State, Writers of Ten Plus Books, Author/Illustrators, and so on.

Author Interest Groups

Divide the class into groups with each group responsible for reading and discussing three books of a particular author. Set up a timetable for completing the books, journal activities, author awareness questions, and so on. Give plenty of time for group meetings and tell the students to take turns leading the discussion.

Newbery Club

Research and discuss the history of the the Newbery Medal. Display several Newbery Medal books. For extra credit, students may read these books. On an 8½ × 11 paper, draw a medal; make several photocopies. After completing a book conference, author awareness activity, or book reaction, the student colors in one-third of the medal. After reading three books, the student becomes a member of the Newbury Club and is granted special privileges throughout the term.

THE COMPLETE LIST OF
NEWBERY WINNERS, 1959–1995

1996	*The Midwife's Apprentice* by Karen Cushman (Clarion)	
1995	*Walk Two Moons* by Sharon Creech (HarperCollins)	
1994	*The Giver* by Lois Lowry (Houghton Mifflin)	
1993	*Missing May* by Cynthia Rylant (Orchard)	
1992	*Shiloh* by Phyllis Reynolds Naylor (Dell)	
1991	*Maniac Magee* by Jerry Spinelli (Little)	

1990   *Number the Stars* by Lois Lowry (Houghton)
1989   *Joyful Noise: Poems for Two Voices* by Paul Fleischman (Harper and Row)
1988   *Lincoln: A Photobiography* by Russell Freedman (Clarion)
1987   *The Whipping Boy* by Sid Fleischman (Greenwillow)
1986   *Sarah, Plain and Tall* by Patricia MacLachlan (Harper Jr.)
1985   *The Hero and the Crow* by Robin McKinley (Greenwillow)
1984   *Dear Mr. Henshaw* by Beverly Cleary (Morrow)
1983   *Dicey's Song* by Cynthia Voight (Atheneum)
1982   *A Visit to William Blake's Inn: Poems for Innocent and Experienced
        Travelers* by Nancy Willard (Harcourt)
1981   *Jacob I Have Loved* by Katherine Paterson (Crowell)
1980   *A Gathering of Days: A New England Girl's Journal, 1830–32* by Joan W.
        Blos (Scribner)
1979   *The Westing Game* by Ellen Raskin (Dutton)
1978   *Bridge to Terabithia* by Katherine Paterson (Crowell)
1977   *Ross of Thunder Hear My Cry* by Mildred D. Taylor (Dial)
1976   *The Grey King* by Susan Cooper (Atheneum)
1975   *M. C. Higgins the Great* by Virginia Hamilton (Macmillan)
1974   *The Slave Dancer* by Paula Fox (Bradbury)
1973   *Julie of the Wolves* by Jean Craighead George (Harper)
1972   *Mrs. Frisby and the Rats of NIMH* by Robert C. O'Brien (Atheneum)
1971   *Summer of the Swans* by Betsy Byars (Viking)
1970   *Sounder* by William H. Armstrong (Pantheon)
1969   *The High King* by Lloyd Alexander (Holt)
1968   *From the Mixed-Up Files of Mrs. Basil E. Frankweiler* by E. L. Konigsburg
        (Atheneum)
1967   *Up a Road Slowly* by Irene Hunt (Follet)
1966   *I Juan de Parega* by Elizabeth Borton de Trevino (Farrar)
1965   *Shadow of a Bull* by Maia Wojciechowska (Atheneum)
1964   *It's Like This, Cat* by Emily Neville (Harper)
1963   *A Wrinkle in Time* by Madeleine L'Engle (Farrar)
1962   *The Bronze Bow* by Elizabeth George Speare (Houghton)
1961   *Island of the Blue Dolphins* by Scott O'Dell (Houghton)
1960   *Onion John* by Joseph Krumgold (Crowell)
1959   *The Witch of Blackbird Pond* by Elizabeth George Speare (Houghton)

Meeting the Author

*They stood on their ledge tucked beneath a rock buttress on the [mountain's] West Ridge
and chatted as they broke down and packed away the camera gear. Theirs was a com-
manding view down three thousand feet to the green cow pastures....Where was the helicopter to lift them off? They stood side by side, less than an arm's length apart.... Dave
opened his mouth to speak. Suddenly both of them heard a faint* whirring *from above—
not the* whirr *of a helicopter, but the whistle of a rock fall.... Instantly Mike dove into the
side, huddling into a small ball.... The ledge exploded in a cloud of flying shards of rock.
In seconds all was quiet again. Mike opened and turned to see Dave at his side. Dave's
safety helmet and the top of his head were gone. Death had been instantaneous. So swift,
only a trickle of blood oozed from what was left of his head. It was as if the life had been
vacuumed out. Even in death Dave's steel-gray eyes bore out at Mike, his pursed lips still
holding the word they would never release. (Taylor, 1981)*

My students and I had never heard of alpinist Rob Taylor before he came to
speak at Brown Junior High. We were entranced the moment he began his adven-
turous tale of tackling a remote mountain peak in the Soviet Union. After Taylor's

dynamic lecture and slide show, my students bombarded him with questions. We were the last class to leave the auditorium and Mr. Taylor gave us an autographed copy of his book *The Breach* with a personal inscription. The children were quite impressed and proudly showed the book to other teachers and students who had missed the lecture. These so-called reluctant readers walked away from the visit with not only new information but also a better understanding of why someone may choose to write a book. They saw Rob Taylor as more than just a writer, but as a real person who does interesting things.

The book is a story of adventure, spiritual challenge, and survival that takes the reader to the 19,000-foot summit of Mt. Kilimanjaro. It is unlikely that any of my students would have picked up this book had they not met the amazing person behind the story. Taylor is not a writer of young adult books and *The Breach* is above the reading level of my students.

"Would you read it to us, Ms. Krieger?" the children asked when we returned to our classroom. And of course I was only happy to oblige. I chose engaging sections to read aloud each day, leaving off at a cliffhanger (literally!). This motivated students to check out the book themselves during silent reading time.

One year, all the seventh- and eighth-graders read Yoko Kawashima Watkin's autobiography, *So Far from the Bamboo Grove*. This simply written book is an account of Yoko's escape from Korea to Japan during World War II. Themes of survival, family unity, prejudice, and war are woven in an engaging tale. My students liked the book, yet its remote setting and incredible tales of survival made the story almost unbelievable. My students asked again and again if the story was really true. Several expressed disbelief that anyone could survive such an ordeal as walking for one month or trekking for days in deep snow.

How fortunate we were that our librarian arranged Yoko Kawashima to visit. Yoko spoke to three separate groups, which allowed a more intimate meeting. A hush came over the children as Yoko entered the library dressed in her kimono. The soft-spoken author described the moment she decided to write down her childhood war experience. She spoke passionately about her family, her homeland, and world peace. The students' hands waved in the air. Now they could ask the questions that had intrigued them so during the past months.

Yoko's visit was an inspiration to teachers as well as students. Over the years, there were other memorable visits from Paul Zindel, Katherine Paterson, Ashley Bryan, and Walter Dean Myers. Children always enjoy meeting a famous person. Unlike sports and movie stars, popular authors are usually invisible. The act of writing is solitary. Meeting the face behind the words is the ultimate in author awareness. Author visits have inspired countless school children to write their own stories and read more books.

Arranging to have a popular author visit your school is not easy. The fee is often high and their visits are booked far in advance. Authors must be paid for their time and effort. Most writers of juvenile books do not become wealthy from their work and cannot afford to travel to schools for free. Seeking support from local businesses, PTAs, councils for the arts, and school budgets are feasible ways to finance an author visit. Don't forget profits from bake sales and book sales, especially sales of the visiting author's books, which can be purchased on consignment at the publisher's discount.

Even if you do not have the funds to secure a well-known author, local writers can be a great resource. Why not invite a sportswriter to your classroom? How about a high school yearbook editor or a TV script writer? Students need to see that learning to write effectively not only boosts their academic performance but it also enhances employment opportunities. Let your students meet real people writing about real things in the real world.

GUIDELINES FOR A SUCCESSFUL AUTHOR VISIT

1. Try to invite an author who would most intrigue your students. Begin with a few in mind. Contact other schools, libraries, and bookstores that have used the author before. Look for authors who receive high recommendations in relating to groups of children. Plan on contacting the author at least *six months in advance.*

2. Authors are most easily reached through their publishers. Direct your inquiries to the library services department or promotion department. State the name of the author, possible dates for the visit, the program format and type of audience, and ask for the fee. (If you know ahead of time how much money is available, say so.)

3. Once an agreement is made, make sure to get all details of the visit—such as travel arrangements, lodging, number of sessions, and bad weather plans—in writing.

4. In most cases, a successful author visit depends on the students' familiarity with his or her books. Allow teachers, librarians, and students ample time to prepare for the author's visit. Try to have multiple copies of the author's books available.

5. Schedule and organize the visit wisely and realistically. Do not fill the auditorium with the entire school. Consider the range of interest, appropriate age level, and familiarity with the author when deciding which students would gain the most from the author's visit.

6. Give the author explicit directions to the school and a warm welcome. Review the schedule and other arrangements. Make sure all equipment is on hand (books, projector, tape recorder, chairs, microphones, etc.).

7. Encourage students to think of questions in advance. Discourage them from asking questions that could easily be answered by reading the book jacket. Students should be told of behavioral expectations beforehand, not after the author is introduced.

8. If the author has agreed to give autographs, allow plenty of time for this.

9. After the scheduled sessions, spend time talking with the author over refreshments or lunch. This is the time to pay the author and to get feedback on the success of the visit. A follow-up letter to the author and publisher is a polite gesture. Children often enjoy writing thank-you notes as well.

10. Think about ways to improve future visits. Start planning your invitation of the next author you'd like to speak to your school.

When Melissa was in fifth grade, she received a letter from children's writer Natalie Babbitt. Two years later, in the midst of author awareness activities in my Reading Workshop, Melissa brought this letter to the class. "You can show your other classes, Ms. Krieger, but be real careful!" she said. From the delicate way Melissa handled the envelope, I could see how much the letter meant to her. "Look," said Melissa, "she even gave me her home address."

In her letter to Natalie Babbitt, Melissa expressed an interest in becoming a writer. Ms. Babbitt sent a "bio" sheet along with a handwritten letter of encouragement. I do not know if this author answers all her fan mail, but this kind gesture made an impact on my student.

Authors such as Katherine Paterson and Judy Blume receive thousands of fan letters each year. If they answered all of them, they wouldn't have time to write books (not to mention the expense of such an endeavor). Beverly Cleary says that over the years, the letters she receives have become more illegible and impolite. Students have asked her for free books and answers for school assignments. One student said she would get an F if Ms. Cleary did not write back! Judy Blume receives so many letters from depressed and confused young people that she published these letters along with her answers and advice in a book called *Letters to Judy: What Your Kids Wish They Could Tell You* (Putnam, 1986).

Well-intentioned teachers may assign their students to write authors without realizing the volume of mail a particular author receives. Also, when teachers do not read the letters beforehand, authors will continue to find inappropriate questions and remarks in the mailbox. Consider these guidelines the next time your students write an author:

1. Think about the popularity of the author. Encourage your students to write new or less famous authors. Help them to understand how many children read Judy Blume's books. Ask them to imagine what it would be like to receive 5,000 fan letters each year.

2. Discourage children from asking questions such as "How many books have you written?" or "Where did you grow up?" Such questions can easily be answered by looking in the library. Children's authors *want* to hear reactions to their books. Help your students express their feelings and thoughts about the characters, plot, and events, rather than just saying "I thought your book was real good." If they have had practice answering author awareness questions, this should not be a problem.

3. Since the students are writing for an audience, stress the importance of legible handwriting, proper spelling, and clarity.

4. Always enclose a self-addressed, stamped envelope.

Real Letters

Here is a terrific book that not only gives children effective models of engaging letters to authors but also develops author awareness: *Dear Author: Students Write about the Books That Change Their Lives* edited by Catherine Gourly (Conari Press, 1995). This collection is a result of a national essay contest sponsored by *READ* magazine (*Weekly Reader*) inviting students in grades 6 through 12 to write "a personal letter to the author of a book that has in some way changed the students' way of thinking." You will not find any dry plot summaries or "the book was so exciting!" in this collection. Here are extremely intimate, heart-felt, letters written in vivid language. There is a wide range of author representation, too, including Charles Dickens, Carl Lewis, Anne Frank, and Shel Silverstein. This is a simple, elongated paperback that students will enjoy browsing through. (The publisher also offers a free teacher's guide with the purchase of the book.)

Following is an example of a letter written to an author from a Reading Workshop student:

Dear Mr. Zindel,

Before I read your book, The Pigman, *I never really liked reading. My teacher told me I'd be laughing as soon as I opened the book. She was right. You sure know how to hook me. I liked John the best because he's a lot like me. I don't like school either, and I have been known to cause trouble. I wouldn't mind having a vocabulary like John though, because then I wouldn't have to learn so many words in my Reading class! For my next book project I'll be reading the sequel to* The Pigman. *If I like that one, I might try your others which have weird titles.*

Sincerely,

"Kenny," Brown Junior High School

References

Blume, Judy. (1986). *Letters to Judy: What Your Kids Wish They Could Tell You.* New York: Putnam.

Duncan, Lois. (1982). *Chapters: My Growth as a Writer.* Boston: Little, Brown, p. 5.

Elliot, Jeffrey M. (Ed.) (1988). *Conversations with Maya Angelou.* University, MS: University of Mississippi.

Gallo, Donald R. (1990). *Speaking for Ourselves.* Urbana, IL: NCTE.

Hinton, S. E. (1967). *The Outsiders.* New York: Viking.

Krull, Kathleen. (1994). *Lives of the Writers: Comedies, Tragedies (and What the Neighbors Thought.* Ill. by Kathryn Hewitt. New York: Harcourt Brace.

Lloyd, Pamela. (1987). *How Writers Write.* Portsmouth, NH: Heinemann.

Melton, David. (1986). *How to Capture Live Authors and Bring Them to Your School.* Kansas City, MO: Landmark.

Murray, Donald M. (1990). *Shoptalk: Learning to Write with Writers.* Portsmouth, NH: Heinemann, p. xiv.

Singer, Isaac Bashevis. (1984). *Stories for Children.* New York: Farrar.

Taylor, Rob. (1981). *The Breach.* New York: Putnam.

6

Lifetime Readers

*By focusing exclusively on drill and skill in the reading process, we
had created schooltime readers instead of lifetime readers.*
—Jim Trelease (1986)

The Book Report Battle

Each September when I address a new crop of Reading Workshop students, someone always asks the big question: "Uh, Ms. Krieger, do we gotta do book reports?"

Most of my students have had loathed doing book reports—even more than taking tests. This is why I have rethought the whole concept of book reports. I asked
myself, Why should secondary students do them? What role do book reports play in
improving reading and writing? How do they accommodate a reader with disabilities? What alternatives can be offered that extend a student's thinking about books?
Does book reporting affect a student's attitude toward reading?

If book reports are a part of your curriculum, ask yourself the same questions.
How confident are you with your answers? Survey other teachers and you may hear
the following responses.

1. Book reports teach students how to summarize information, which is an
   essential writing/comprehension skill.
2. Book reports encourage students to reflect on their reading.
3. Book reporting gives students practice in identifying literary devises such as
   plot, setting, and theme.
4. Book reports are a way of getting students to read and for teachers to know
   if a student has read a particular book.
5. Book reports are usually part of the high school English class. Therefore, students need to be familiar with the format.

The first three responses may be true, but I would argue that there are many
other creative and enjoyable ways to teach those skills. Many English and reading
teachers have discovered this already, and there are a number of resources available
that offer unique alternatives to book reporting. Some of these activities include
making book jackets with blurbs, giving book talks, performing character interviews,
designing collages, keeping response journals, forming classroom book clubs, and
doing author awareness activities.

The fourth reason for book reporting is a poor one. After all, it does not take
much ingenuity to know when a student has really read a book. And when was the

last time you heard a student say, "Boy, after writing that book report I couldn't wait to read another book!"? Yes, assigning book reports may *force* a student to read, but research shows that it too often squelches a child's desire to read independently.

In the book, *Voices of Readers* by G. Robert Carlsen and Anne Sherrill (1988), college students across the country reflect on their school reading experiences. One overwhelming sentiment was the hatred of book reports. The frequency of this assignment turned some students off to reading. Selecting short or easy books (or books they had already read) was a popular way to approach the task. Many students expressed frustration with having to think of something clever or insightful to say. (Most wrote what they thought their teacher wanted to hear.) One of them reported, "I loved to read just for the sake of reading and learning something new. But reading came to mean remembering insignificant details in order to make a book report—reading in order to get a grade and to fulfill a requirement" (p. 102).

Another problem with book reports is that good readers almost always do them well and poor readers rarely do them well, because poor readers are never great writers and often have difficulty with organizing and summarizing information. They may lack the vocabulary to actually talk about a book. How many times have you come across generic comments like these in a book report: "It was a really great book!" "It had lots of action." "I would recommend it to anyone who likes mysteries."

My classroom population usually consists of a few students who enjoy reading but who have difficulty with higher-level comprehension, many students who read only for school, and some students who do not read at all. I have found that assigning book reports frustrates the first group, discourages the second group, and perpetuates the I-hate-to-read attitude in the third.

Although I do not assign book reports in my classroom, I think it is worthwhile having your students do one (not four)—if only because they will have to do them with other teachers. I have found the following guidelines to optimize learning and opportunities for success with book reporting.

1. Always provide a model of a good report as well as a poor report before students begin writing. Have students identify the strengths and weaknesses in each report.
2. Offer students a list of sentence starters to develop their observations and commentary. Examples are: One part I found confusing was…, The author did a particularly great job with…, The most interesting character is…, The message in the story seems to be….
3. Show students how to spice up their reports using quotations, strong verbs, or an attention-grabbing lead.

I view book reporting as a writing exercise, but an artificial one. Ask students why they have to do reports and you'll most likely hear, "So the teacher can know if we really read it." Using the book report as a stepping stone to the book review, a form of writing that actually exists outside the classroom, makes the assignment more meaningful to students. Have them study reviews from ewspapers and magazines first in order to teach the characteristics of this genre. Students can then submit their own reviews to youth magazines such as *U.S. Kids* and *Creative Kids* or make a classroom publication.

One drawback is that book reviews are difficult to write. If students have not mastered certain rudimentary reading/writing skills they will experience trouble moving beyond summarizing. It may be difficult for some of us to give up assigning book reports. After all, they have been around a long time. We had to do reports when we were in school. Parents expect them (and some principals do, too). Yet, your students will not be book reporting outside the classroom or in college. They will not find a collection of book reports in the bookstore. They will not cherish their reports in years to come. Nor will they grow to love reading through writing book reports. Yes, they *may* become good at writing them; they *may* become better at summarizing stories and identifying literary terms; and they *may* even derive a sense of accomplishment from a job well done. However, in this busy electronic age, adolescents are doing less reading for pleasure. So the questions remains: If our goal is to encourage life-long reading habits, how do we proceed? In *Voices of Readers*, students tell us the answer: Share a love of books; read aloud regularly; and provide uninterrupted time to read during class, access to a variety of books, opportunities for choice, and interesting follow-up activities.

If you work with poor readers, you know that getting them to write *anything* is a struggle. As many creative ideas as I have come up with to replace book reports, there are always a few disgruntled students who take three months to finish a book in an attempt to avoid extension activities. Sometimes it is refreshing just to let the children read and talk freely about their books. (Imagine!) I learned this from James, a seventh-grader, when he asked me, "Hey, can I just finish the book or do I still have to do more chapter questions? I'm really at the exciting part and I want to finish it." And indeed, he did—two days later. And the class heard James's rave review.

The Classroom Library

Do you have a classroom *bookshelf* or a classroom *library?* Bookshelves gather dust; libraries gather readers. I have found that children gravitate toward book displays. They like to see the covers. For many young readers, such an encounter with books is less intimidating than a huge, unorganized bookshelf. I always have a few books displayed on my desk or on the shelf under a bulletin board. The display books share a common thread: theme, genre, author, or subject. I look for books that tie in current events, sports, holidays, and history. Books that youngsters can browse through, particularly nonfiction, make good display titles. One of the most popular displays has been games, puzzles, and brainteaser books.

I also have a large standing bookshelf for browsing and borrowing. I prefer to keep the books grouped by author. This forces kids to pay attention to the authors' names and cuts down on filing errors. A sign-out sheet is the simplest procedure for borrowing books, but if you are really organized, you might try putting pocket cards in each book. Students could also be in charge of running the classroom library.

Middle school students prefer books that are not tattered and torn. I have adopted the practice of reinforcing the spine and cover edges with clear tape. I enlist the help of students for this preventive measure, which extends the life of paperbacks quite a bit. In addition, I expect my students to treat books with care. If a brand new book comes back dirty or torn, I ask the student to replace it.

Most of my classroom budget is spent on trade books. Library and rummage sales are great sources for cheap books. By getting to know the librarian at my town library, I have received free books and magazines that would otherwise be thrown out. Used books stores, outlets, and discount tables are other good places to find bargains. Book clubs such as Troll or Scholastic offer students inexpensive, high-interest selections. Teachers receive points for the number of orders and can use them for free books.

Learning to Use (and Love) the Library

In the book *Once Upon a Time...*(Trelease, 1986), authors Natalie Babbitt, Judy Blume, and Arnold Lobel write about their childhood love of the library. After my mother, my town library was the second biggest influence in my becoming a reader. I loved the smell of the books, the inviting arrangement of small tables and chairs, and the cheerful librarians who stamped my stack of books. Unfortunately, I did not have the same feeling toward my elementary school librarian, who threatened us if a book was overdue and spent more time spying gum-chewing kids than enticing us with books.

Young people need to feel welcomed in the library. They need comfortable places to read, work, and whisper. They like cozy corners, couches, book displays, posters, magazines, listening stations, and computer terminals. Middle school students in their self-conscious, awkward stage need librarians who treat them with respect, connect them with books and authors, and help them find information without being condescending.

At the beginning of the school year, our junior high school librarian always gave a student orientation. A few classes would pile in the library to hear a thorough lecture on locating books, book categorization, identifying reference texts, and so on. This approach did not work for my Reading Workshop students. They grew restless and did not retain even half of what was said. I found I needed to do my own orientation in small bits throughout the first half of the year. I begin by finding out what experiences my students have had with libraries. Then I ask: What services and information can a library provide? What do you want from the school library?

Rather than quizzing the youngsters on reference skills, I take an informal inventory.

Suppose you want a book by Judy Blume, what do you do?
How can you find a map of Japan?
What are those numbers for on the spine of books?
Where would you look for a book on soccer?

Just as I try to teach reading and writing skills in context, I try to cover library skills in the same manner. For example, when my students were researching authors' lives, I introduced them to the various references available, such as the *Something about the author* series.

A good working relationship with your school librarian is essential to your classroom program. Let your librarian know your needs. Give advance notice on what topics your class will study. During the author project, our librarian filled a book cart with several biographies for me to use in my classroom.

Helping Students Select Books

If we continually dictate what our students must read, then how will they ever learn to develop their own literary tastes? Extensive research by Donald Graves (1983), Nancie Atwell (1987), and Kenneth Goodman (1984) demonstrate the impact of giving students choices about their reading. There is no one book that will reach all youngsters. Each reader has different needs and interests that cannot be met and addressed through teacher-dictated curriculum. Furthermore, the wide range of abilities in students is all the more reason to give them choices in what they read.

This does not mean you should not read books as a class or assign a short story for homework. Just make sure your students feel they have some degree of choice, particularly in their outside reading. Provide readers with book lists from which to choose selections. Create a genre chart that students complete after reading one book in each category. In my Famous Authors course, students researched an author of their choice and were required to read one work by that writer. If your English curriculum is school mandated, then do not pile on additional assigned reading. Give your students plenty of opportunity for self-selected pleasure reading.

In this context of choice, you can still lead children to certain books and authors. I like to surprise my students with books commercials. "This lesson is being brought to you by Gary Paulsen's novel, *Tracker.*" I whet my students' appetites with Book Bits—reading aloud intriguing, exciting, or funny passages. Another technique that I have seen demonstrated is the Book Talk. The teacher (or librarian) assumes the role of the book's main character and performs a monologue for the class. This takes more preparation but is quite effective. After our librarian did a Book Talk on Robert Lipsyte's *The Contender*, there were more eager readers than copies of the book.

Another way to direct youngsters to books they will enjoy is to create lists based on student favorites. Middle school students like to know what books their peers find interesting. I keep a file box called "Readers' Reviews." When students finish a book they especially enjoyed, I encourage them to fill out a card listing their name, the book title, author, number of pages, and a one-sentence plug. Nancie Atwell (1987), author of *In the Middle*, asks her students to rate the books they have read on a scale of 1 to 10. Atwell then compiles a list, based on the highest ratings, for next year's class.

Book ownership is also an important part of literacy development. I keep books on hand to give as prizes and presents. Throughout the school year, I hold a few class book swaps. Every so often, I send parents a list of book gift ideas. Try a field trip to a local bookstore. Students could learn about the operation of a bookstore as well as the new titles available, and then have time for browsing and buying.

As Jim Trelease (1986) reminds us in his introduction to *Once Upon a Time:*

> *It is today's children who are so touched by the joy of reading who in turn will share it with another generation years from now, when they themselves become parents or teachers or maybe even authors. And the more such shared beginnings, the less likely the joy of reading will ever end.*

Marishka was a seventh-grade student from Russia whose father wanted her to drop the English-as-a-Second-Language (ESL) classes and take regular English. As a compromise, the guidance counselor placed Marishka with me in Reading Workshop. I had no training in ESL and was uncertain how much I should expect from Marishka. She spoke rapidly with a heavy accent, yet her English vocabulary, both receptive and expressive, seemed strong. Reading and writing English was another matter. Marishka's reading rate was very slow. Her handwriting was illegible, and not surprisingly, she had a lot of trouble with spelling and grammar.

Marishka enjoyed talking with me before and after class time, but in class, she seemed uninterested in the contemporary short stories we were reading and put little effort into related assignments. I searched for high-interest easy novels for Marishka to read which she dutifully completed without much enthusiasm. After a few weeks, I could tell Marishka was unhappy in my class.

One day, I spotted Marishka in the cafeteria during lunch. She sat alone engrossed in a thick, hardcover book. "What are you reading?" I asked.

Marishka looked up and smiled. "Dostoyevski. Have you heard of him?" She handed me the book.

As I flipped through the pages, the Russian words blurred together. I sat down next to this unusual child and smiled. "Okay, so tell me about Dostoyevski."

I learned a lesson that day. Here was a very bright girl, who, in her native tongue, read fluently and at college level. Here was a girl who had a passion for the classics, mythology, politics, and Russian poetry. And I hadn't known this! No wonder she was bored in my class. Marishka had little interest in the contemporary adolescent novels my students enjoyed. She obviously had no trouble with reading comprehension either, unlike my other students.

Upon discovering Marishka's intellectual strengths and private literary world, I was able to modify and enrich her Reading Workshop program. Together with Marishka, I worked out a plan. She could read her beloved Russian novels at home, then complete the author awareness activities and book projects in English.

I also found audio recordings of poetry reading and classic books for Marishka to listen to while reading along. This motivated her to read more English books, and, after several weeks, there was a considerable improvement in her reading rate. For alternative assignments, I sometimes used short newspaper and magazine articles on current events (another of her interests). When I could, I met individually with Marishka to work on points of English grammar and spelling.

Marishka grew happier as her abilities and interests were acknowledged and respected. She taught me that I must not let language barriers cause me to make assumptions about academic and intellectual abilities. Teachers must strive to be sensitive to the cultural differences students bring to the classroom, and our literature should reflect this.

References

Atwell, Nancie. (1987). *In the Middle: Writing, Reading, and Learning with Adolescents.* Portsmouth, NH: Heinemann.

Carlsen, Robert G., & Sherrill, Anne. (1988). *Voices of Readers: How We Come to Love Books.* Urbana, IL: NCTE.

Goodman, Kenneth. (1984). Unity in reading. In A. Purves and O. Niles (Eds.), *Becoming Readers in a Complex Society* (Part 1). 83rd Yearbook of the National Society for the Study of Education. Chicago: University of Chicago Press.

Graves, D. H. (1983). *Writing: Teachers and Children at Work.* Portsmouth, NH: Heinemann.

Krieger, Evelyn. (1991). The book report battle. *The Journal of Reading, 35,* 340–341.

Trelease, Jim. (1986). Introduction. *Once Upon Time....* New York: G. P. Putnam's Sons, p. 11.

Trelease, Jim. (1993). Introduction. *Read All about It.* New York: Penguin, p. xi.

Multicultural Short Stories

Hamilton, Virginia. (1985). *The People Could Fly.* Ill. by Leo and Diane Dillon. New York: Knopf.
Humorous and inspirational African American folktales kept alive by slave tellers.

Hamilton, Virginia. (1993). *Many Thousand Gone: African Americans from Slavery to Freedom.* Ill. by Leo and Diane Dillon. New York: Knopf.

Mazer, Anne. (Ed.). (1993). *America Street: A Multicultural Anthology of Stories.* New York: Persea Books.

Singer, Isaac B. (1984). *Zlateh the Goat and Other Stories.* Ill. by Maurice Sendak. New York: Harper.
Seven folktales derived from the eastern European Jewish oral tradition.

Soto, Gary. (1990). *Baseball in April and Other Stories.* San Diego: Harcourt.
These delightful stories will especially appeal to boys and make good read-alouds.

Tate, Eleanor E. (1992). *Front Porch Stories at the One-Room School.* New York: Bantam.
These stories have a distinct voice and make great read-alouds. The author is former president of the National Association of Black Storytellers.

Short Story Collections

Aiken, Joan. (1980). *Touch of Chill.* New York: Delacorte.
Real page-turners in this collection!

Cormier, Robert. (1991). *Eight Plus One.* New York: Dell.
The introduction to each story by the author make it particularly good for author awareness and budding writers.

Elwood, Roger (Ed.). (1973). *Science Fiction Tales: Invaders, Creatures, and Alien Worlds.* Chicago: Rand Mcnally.
Well suited for grades 4–6.

Westall, Robert. (1992). *In Camera and Other Stories.* New York: Scholastic.
Five enjoyable supernatural tales. Especially good for older students who do not read well.

Yolen, Jane, & Greenberg, Martin H. (Eds.). (1989). *Things That Go Bump in the Night: A Collection of Original Stories.* New York: Harper and Row, 1989.

Great Books for Boys

Aaseng, Nate. (1983). "You Are the Coach" series. New York: Dell, Lerner.

These books place readers in coaching situations where they must decide the best move. Covers basketball, hockey, football, and baseball.

Ansell, Rod, & Percy, Rachel. (1986). *To Fight the Wild.* New York: Harcourt.
After a boating accident, Ansell is stranded in Australia's Northern Territory and must use his knowledge of bush lore to survive. A good read-aloud.

Dygard, Thomas J. (1986). *Halfback Tough.* New York: Morrow.
Football turns a young boy's life around. Also by the same author: *Outside Shooter, Soccer Duel,* and *Winning Kicker.*

Mazer, Harry. (1979). *The Last Mission.* New York: Dell.
A teenage boy eager to experience the excitement and glory of war enlists in the World War II Army Air Corps using false identification. What he finds is not what he expects.

Paulsen, Gary. (1987). *Hatchet.* New York: Bradbury.
A young teenage boy survives the Canadian wilderness after a plane crash.

Paulsen, Gary. (1991). *The River.* New York: Delacorte.
The sequel to *Hatchet.*

Great Books for Girls

Furlong, Monica. (1987). *Wise Child.* New York: Knopf.
A fantasy about a young girl in a Scottish village who is adopted by a sorceress.

Hendry, Frances Mary. (1992). *Quest for a Maid.* New York: Farrar.
A classic thirteenth-century adventure story full of unforgettable characters.

Montgomery, Lucy Maude. (1992). *Anne of Green Gables.* Bantam.1992.
Many of your students will have seen the wonderful video adaptation of this classic story and may be motivated to try the book and its sequels. The author's life makes a great read as well.

Paterson, Katherine. (1991). *Lyddie.* New York: Puffin.
A story of a factory girl working in a textile mill who becomes a heroine.

Smith, Betty. (1968). *A Tree Grows in Brooklyn.* New York: Perennial Library.
A bittersweet growing up story of 11-year-old Francie Nolan full of hopes and dreams.

Epilogue

There they stood in front of class after class, books clutched to their bosoms (as if to say, "Mine, Mine!"), calling on me when I did not have my hand raised, probing for, insisting on, the one and only right answer to questions they posed—answers they already knew and wouldn't tell the class until we'd been sufficiently humbled, convinced that because we could not read their minds, we could not read.

—Sandy Asher (1992)

For several years, I have privately tutored children of all ages and abilities in reading, writing, and study skills. This work had a great impact on my own classroom teaching. Outside the school setting, with a neutral teacher who does not grade or reprimand them, children open up and take more risks. They are willing to struggle, to fall, and to show their vulnerabilities. I, in turn, am given a window to their thinking and learning. Why is it they failed the history test? Why do they wait until the last moment to write the book report? Why don't they read for pleasure?

Sometimes, I am impressed by an assignment they show me, or a teacher's comment, or the literature they read in school. But, more often than not, I am depressed. Why? Because during my 12 years of tutoring, I still see far too much teacher-directed learning ("chalk talk"), far too much memorizing and testing, and so little reading aloud and student-selected literature. I feel my students' humiliation at not reading well, their fear of 300-page assigned books, and their despair when their writing is attacked by the red pen.

The distaste for reading can be developed by well-intentioned teachers. Here is my recipe for taking the flavor out of reading.

1. Make sure to assign books that you think the children should read. The Great Books of the Western World should feature prominently on the required reading list.
2. If you do allow the children to select a book, make sure it is preapproved and not written by an author of questionable worth.
3. Don't waste time reading *to* the students. The books were written for them to read.
4. Check that students are doing the required reading by giving regular chapter quizzes. Check comprehension by assigning several questions to be answered for each chapter.
5. Give lists of vocabulary words from the book for students to look up and memorize.

6. Ask students to write compositions on topics related to the book such as: What does the book really means? Make sure students know that there are right and wrong answers. Grade their papers.
7. Assign book reports—the more, the better.
8. Ask students to analyze poems and short stories. Dismantle the literature into small parts. Test them on this.
9. Stand in front of the class or behind your desk. Have students sit in rows and do most of the listening. Ask a lot of questions. Call on students to check their understanding.
10. Make sure class discussions stick to the predetermined topic.

In her radical book, *Real Lives: Eleven Teenagers Who Don't Go to School*, Grace Llewellyn (1993) presents self-written profiles of home-schooled teens. One girl says, "One of the reasons I continue to learn at home is because I love to read. All of my friends who go to school hate to read."

What a sad statement! School learning should not lead to a distaste for reading. All children start out with a longing for stories. In the words of writer Daniel Pennac (1994), "The child drinks them in as he drinks his milk." Books are pleasurable, exciting, colorful, interesting, and funny. The child's early teachers, mainly his parents, are the beloved storytellers, not the reading police whom the child may encounter later on in school who question, prod, push, analyze, demand, and test.

Certainly school is not the only source of blame for children who do not read. Life today is more visual, electronic, and fast paced. Television, movies, popular music, computer games, sports, and peers all compete for children's attention. Add to this parents who have stopped reading to their children or who do not read themselves. These outside influences make the reading classroom even more essential. Our children desperately need teachers who can instill a desire to read, who can seduce youngsters with stories, and who can breathe life into books.

We cannot force reading. We cannot *teach* a love of reading. We can only foster this love by creating an atmosphere in which it will grow. If it grows, the youngsters will read. If they like to read, they will read more. They will learn, think, and develop skills. They may become more willing to sweat the bigger stuff like Dickens and Shakespeare.

What is this atmosphere? It is an atmosphere surrounded by books and periodicals of all kinds. It is a place where students have a voice in discussions and whose interpretations are valued. It is a place where students have plenty of opportunity to select their books. It is a place where students can, once again, hear the beloved storyteller as the teacher always makes time to read aloud. There is class time, too, for silent reading. The reading list contains both modern, classic, and multicultural selections. It is a place where a variety of literature-related activities happen, such as dramatization, author study, and journal writing. It is a place where the teacher, as a guide rather than the Supreme Authority, helps the students hear what the author whispers.

I leave you with the eloquent words of writer and teacher Anne Lammot, author of *Bird by Bird* (Pantheon, 1994), addressing her college students' question, Why does reading and writing matter?

Because for some of us, books are as important as almost anything else on earth. What a miracle it is that out of these small, flat, rigid squares of paper unfolds world after world after world, worlds that sing to you, comfort and quiet or excite you. Books help us understand who we are and how we are to behave. They show us what community and friendship mean; they show us how to live and die. They are full of all the things that you don't get in real life—wonderful lyrical language, for instance, right off the bat. And quality of attention: we may notice amazing details during the course of a day but we rarely let our-selves stop and really pay attention. An author makes you notice, makes you pay attention, and this is a great gift. My gratitude for good writing is unbounded; I'm grateful for it the way I'm grateful for the ocean. Aren't you? I ask. (p. 15)

References

Asher, Sandy. (1992). Ride the Horse in the Direction It's Going, in Donald R. Gallo (Ed.), *Author Insights: Turning Teenagers Into Readers & Writers* (p. 14). Portsmouth, NH: Heinemann.

Lammot, Anne. (1994). *Bird by Bird.* New York: Pantheon.

Llewellyn, Grace. (1993). *Eleven Teenagers Who Don't Go to School.* Eugene, OR: Lowry.

Pennac, Daniel. (1994). *Better Than Life.* Trans. David Homel. Toronto: Coach House Press.

Appendix:
Reading Workshop
Description

Reading Workshop is a year-long course offered in three semesters as an alternative to the larger English and Composition course. The class size of 6 to 12 students (with an average of 10) allows for small group and individualized instruction. The curriculum is based on the needs and interests of the students, as well as the current school English curriculum. Much freedom and flexibility is granted to the teacher in the design and content of the course.

STUDENT PROFILE

Students are recommended by their sixth-grade teacher in the spring following their entrance to junior high school. Students who are unable to keep up in their junior high school English and social studies classes may be recommended for Reading Workshop at various times throughout the year. Students typically experience difficulty in one or more of these areas:

Reading comprehension
Organizational and study skills
Writing ability
Motivation and interest
Understanding and completing assignments

GOALS

Increase motivation for learning.
Promote reading for pleasure.
Explore reading for a variety of purposes.
Develop study/organizational skills.
Learn strategies to aide comprehension.
Improve basic writing skills.

CURRICULUM

Short story reading
Novel study
Author study
Process writing

Nonfiction reading
Content area reading
Developing literary tastes

SPECIFIC SKILLS

Note taking
Organization of notebooks, papers, folders
Keeping track of and completing homework in all classes
Studying for tests

INSTRUCTIONAL AND MANAGEMENT STRATEGIES

Teach students to set goals.
Make opportunities for student self-evaluation.
Help students to monitor their own progress.
Maintain high expectations for all.
Hold brief individual student conferences.
Relate skills learned to other classes and real life.
Allow flexibility and choice in assignments/homework.
Use humor and element of surprise.

A WORD ABOUT HOMEWORK . . .

Over the years, I have had my share of homework battles. The students who needed the extra practice were almost always the ones who rarely did their homework. I have nagged, cajoled, rewarded, and reprimanded; I have called parents; and I have spent hours dreaming up creative or "fun" homework assignments—all this with minimal success. The reasons for not doing homework ranged from being overloaded with work from other classes, family responsibilities, after-school activities, forgetfulness, and lack of motivation and parental assistance. Tracking and grading missing homework assignments took energy away from my teaching. Worst of all, too many class lessons had to be altered because not enough students had completed the homework.

Since I have never been one to threaten or instill fear in my students, I knew I would have to come up with an alternate plan. To simply scrap the notion of homework would send the wrong message. Here was my solution: The homework assignment would always be the same (no excuses about forgetting to write it down or being absent; parents would also know what to expect). Students would be responsible for reading a book of their choice for 20 minutes each school night and to record the number of pages they read. Checking their reading was easily accomplished through a variety of methods: quick, one-on-one conferences; class discussions; a follow-up activity the next day; author awareness questions; and response journals.

A variation of this is to require students to read a minimum of 50 pages a week. This allows students to budget their time. Some enjoy reading all 50 at one sitting, and others find they want to read even more. I have numbered half-inch graph paper from 1 to 300 and made photocopies for each student. Students then color in the number of pages as they read. This was a big hit. The graphs inspired a healthy dose of competition and gave students a visual representation of their efforts. Students who hit the 300 mark are congratulated in front of the class and receive a "culinary treat"—always desirable with this age group.

My homework solution builds reading fluency and concentration, exposes students to a variety of books, allows for individual differences, and promotes reading outside the classroom. Furthermore, it frees the teacher to spend less time correcting and more time creating exciting classes.

Bibliography

Asher, Sandy. (1987). *Where Do You Get Your Ideas?* New York: Walker.
Poet and novelist, Sandy Asher responds to the questions young people ask. She also asks other authors such as Lois Lowry and Ellen Conford to describe the beginnings of their stories. Students will discover the "stories behind the stories" and that many good ideas for books come from personal experience. Poetry and nonfiction is explored as well. Grades 4–8.

Bolton, Sarah. (1952). *Famous American Authors.* New York: Crowell.
Thumbnail biographies of American literary greats such as Thoreau, Poe, Alcott, and Twain. Grades 6 and up.

Cormier, Robert. (1991). *8 Plus 1: Stories.* New York: Dell.
Nine very accessible and touching stories. Each story has a detailed introduction from the author describing where and how the story was created. Robert Cormier's comments on his craft add a new dimension to the stories.

Gallo, Donald R. (Ed.). (1990, 1993). *Speaking for Ourselves: Autobiographical Sketches by Notable Authors of Books for Young Adults* (Volumes 1 and 2). Urbana, IL: National Council of Teachers of English.
Includes photos and fresh, inspiring, and interesting personal information shared through 100 brief sketches. Grades 5 and up.

Hoff, Rhoda. (1969). *Four American Poets: Why They Wrote.* Portland ME: Walch.
Includes Dickinson, Longfellow, Poe, and Whitman. Grades 7 and up.

Hopkins, Bennett Lee. (1969). *Books Are by People.* New York: Citation Press.
Interviews with 104 authors and illustrators of books for young children. Good teacher resource. Grades 4–8.

Kafka, Sherry, & Coles, Robert (Eds.). (1982). *I Will Always Stay Me: Writings of Migrant Children.* Austin: Texas Monthly Press. Grades 5 and up.

Krull, Kathleen. (1994). *The Lives of Writers: Comedies, Tragedies, (and What the Neighbors Thought).* Ill. by Kathryn Hewitt. New York: Harcourt, Brace.
Did you know that Mark Twain wore only white linen suits? Includes 20 lively profiles of famous writers such as Louisa May Alcott, Langston Hughes, and Jack London. Children will enjoy reading the inside scoop on the strange habits, fears, dreams, marriages, and wealth of these literary luminaries. Grades 5–9.

McElmeel, Shannon. (1988). *An Author a Month (for Pennies).* Littleton, CO: Libraries Unlimited.
A unique resource book that features 12 author units. Provides biographies, photographs, and activity suggestions designed to sharpen critical thinking and motivate student reading and writing. Encourages students to discover similarities among themes, styles, and topics employed by different writers. Grades K–6.

Muir, Jane. (1959). *Famous Modern American Women Writers*. New York: Dodd, Mead.

Norby, Shirley, & Ryan, Gregory. (1990). *Famous Children's Authors* (Vols. 1–2). Minneapolis: T. S. Denison.
 Lively and easy-to-read biographical sketches of 20 children's authors such as Dr. Seuss, Beverly Cleary, Maurice Sendak, and Shel Silverstein.

Owens, Richard C. (Publisher). (1993–1994). *Meet the Author Collection*. (New additions currently being published.) 800-336-5588.
 These engaging autobiographical accounts give children a glimpse into the everyday lives of their favorite authors. The simple text reads like a conversation. Children learn where the writers get ideas, where they work, how they edit stories, and how they got started. These 32-page hardcover books are fully photographed in color. Meet Lee Bennet Hopkins, Karla Kuskin, Jean Fritz, and several others. Although written for 7- to 10-year-olds, fifth- and sixth-graders may find these interesting and informative. For junior high students, the books are good examples of autobiographical writing.

Reading Is Fundamental. (1986). *Once Upon a Time*. New York: G.P. Putnam's Sons.
 This beautifully illustrated book features several children's authors reflecting on their childhood days of reading and writing. Selections are short. Grades 1–8.

Smaridge, Norah. (1973). *Famous Author/Illustrators for Young People*. New York: Dodd, Mead.

Southall, Ivan. (1982). *A Journey of Discovery: On Writing for Children*. Austin: Texas Monthly Press.
 An award-winning Australian author traces the development of his talent and books. Grades 4–8.

Weiss, Jerry (Ed.). (1979). *From Writers to Students: The Pleasures and Pains of Writing*. Newark, DE: IRA.
 Interviews with 17 noted writers of adolescent fiction. Includes Lawrence Yep and Judy Blume. Presented in a question/answer format, the interviews are revealing and accessible to young readers.

Contemporary Author Biographies (arranged alphabetically by author of interest)

Maya Angelou

Kallen, Stuart A. (1993). *Maya Angelou: Woman of Words, Deeds and Dreams*. Edina, MN: Abdo & Daughters, 32 pp.
 A well-organized, easy-to-read biography with photographs. Grades 5–8.

Judy Blume

Lee, Betsy. (1981). *Judy Blume's Story*. Minneapolis: Dillion Press.
 A biography with photographs and interesting stories. Grades 4–8.

Pearl Buck

Buck, Pearl. (1954). *My Several Worlds: A Personal Record*. New York: Day. Grades 6–8.

Betsy Byars

Julian, Betsy Byars. (1991). *Besty Byars: The Moon and I*. Englewood Cliffs, NJ: Messner.
 The author of 40-plus books shares her childhood passion for animals and the evolution of her writing career. Funny and very readable. Grades 5–7.

Beverly Cleary

A Girl from Yamhill: A Memoir by Beverly Cleary. NY: Morrow, 1988.
> A fascinating account of Beverly Cleary's childhood which includes several memories that appeared in her books. The author traces her writing career. This sensitive and honest book is an excellent read-aloud. Grades 6–8.

Robert Cormier

Campbell, Patricia J. (1985). *Presenting Robert Cormier.* Boston: Twayne.
> The controversy surrounding the author's books is addressed. His short stories and novels are also analyzed. Grades 7 and up.

Cormier, Robert. (1991). *I Have Words to Spend: Reflections of a Small-Town Editor.* New York: Delacorte.
> In this memoir, an award-winning writer of young adult fiction discusses his life as a newspaper editor and how it relates to his fiction.

Roald Dahl

Dahl, Roald. (1993). *My Year.* New York: Viking, 1993.
> The beloved author of *James and the Giant Peach* recalls his growing up years in a monthly journal of the seasons. Wonderful descriptions of the English countryside. Good model of autobiographical writing. All ages.

Lois Duncan

Duncan, Lois. (1982). *Chapters: My Growth as a Writer.* New York: Little, Brown.
> Detailed account of the author's career (beginning with her first magazine sale at age 13), which includes photographs and samples of early stories and poems. Lois Duncan wrote several teen mystery/adventure novels such as *Down a Dark Hall, Stranger in the Mirror, Ransom,* and *Killing Mr. Griffin. Chapters* is a very engaging autobiography that demonstrates how the writer's life experiences shape her work. Duncan writes in a natural voice that speaks directly to her young readers. Grades 5–8.

Jean Fritz

Fritz, Jean. (1982). *Homesick: My Own Story.* New York: J. P. Putnam.
> Distinguished author of American history nonfiction books for children writes about her childhood in China. The book reads like an adventure novel. Grades 4–8.

S. E. Hinton

Daly, Jay. (1987). *Presenting S. E. Hinton.* New York: Twayne, 1987.
> Part of a biography series. Some of the mystery behind this author is explained. Her four novels are analyzed in terms of plot, characterization, and theme and compared to the film. Grades 7 and up.

Langston Hughes

Meltzer, Milton. (1968). *Langston Hughes: A Biography.* New York: Crown.

M. E. Kerr

Kerr, M. E. (1983). *Me, Me, Me, Me, Not a Novel.* New York: Harper and Row.
> This popular young adult novelist shares her own adolescent experience. Grades 6–9.

Pace, Alleen. (1986). *Presenting M. E. Kerr.* Boston: Twayne.
> A critical study of the author's work and biographical information. Grades 7–10.

Norma Klein

Phy, Allene Stuart. (1988). *Presenting Norma Klein.* Boston: Twayne.
> One of a series of critical study and biographical information. Grades 7–9.

Jean Little

Little, Jean. (1987). *Little by Little: A Writer's Education.* Markham, Ontario: Viking/
Kestrel.
Jean Little tells how her love of reading and books helped her overcome her
visual handicap and influenced her decision to become a writer. Very inspiring.
Grades 4–8.

Ann M. Martin

Becker, Margot, with Martin, Ann M. (1993). *Ann M. Martin: Story of the Author of
the Baby Sitters Club.* New York: Scholastic.
True fans and aspiring writers will be interested in reading this cover to cover.
Teachers may wish to read aloud the chapters on Ann's ideas, babysitting
experiences, and publishing success. Chapter 17, "The Birth of a Super Series,"
is particularly good for illustrating how an idea evolves into a published book.
Grades 4–6.

Milton Meltzer

Meltzer, Milton. (1988). *Starting from Home: A Writer's Beginnings.* Markham,
Ontario: Viking/Kestrel.
A funny and moving memoir of his childhood and teenage years in the early
1900s. Meltzer trace his roots from eastern Europe to New York's Lower East
Side, to Worcester, Massachussets. Students will also gain insight into a rapidly
changing America. Grades 4–8.

Katherine Paterson

Paterson, Katherine. (1981). *Gates of Excellence: On Reading and Writing Books for
Children.* New York: Elsevier/Nelso.
A beautifully written and inspiring book by Newbery Award author Katherine
Paterson (*Jacob I Have Loved, Bridge to Terabithea, The Great Gilly Hopkins*).
Includes her award acceptance speeches. An excellent book for teachers.
Excerpts could be used with grades 7–8, particularly with more sophisticated
readers.

Bill Peet

Peet, Bill. (1989). *Bill Peet: An Autobiography.* Boston: Houghton Mifflin.
This author/illustrator recounts and illustrates his charmed and funny life.
Grades 4–6.

Cynthia Rylant

Rylant, Cynthia. (1982). *When I Was Young in the Mountains.* Ill. by Diane Goode.
New York: Dutton. 32 pp.
A Newbery Honor picture book of Rylant's childhood memories. Great choice
for animal lovers. Film version available from Random House Video, 1986.

Eudora Welty

Welty, Eudora. (1984). *One Writer's Beginnings.* Cambridge, MA: Harvard University
Press.
The best-selling autobiography of the prolific southern writer. Her language is
exquisite. This is a wonderful book for teachers. Selections could be used with
grades 7 and 8, especially with sophisticated readers.

Elizabeth Yates

Yates, Elizabeth. (1981). *Elizabeth Yates: My Diary—My World.* Philadelphia: West-
minster Press.

Authors of the Past

Louisa May Alcott

Anderson, Gretchen (Compiler). (1985). *The Louisa May Alcott Cookbook.* Ill. by K. Milone. Boston: Little, Brown.

Fisher, Aileen & Rabe, Olive. (1969). *We Alcotts: The Story of Louisa May Alcott as Seen through the Eyes of "Marmee," Mother of Little Women.* New York: Antheneum.

MacDonald, Ruth K. (1993). *Louisa May Alcott.* Boston: Twayne. Grades 7–12.

Meigs, Cornelia Lynde. (1968). *Invincible Louisa: The Story of the Author of Little Women.* New York: Little, Brown. Grades 6–8.

Ridlon, Marci. (1988). *Story of Louisa May Alcott: Determined Writer.* New York: Dell Yearling. Grades 2–5.

Ryan, Gary (1993). *Louisa May Alcott: Her Girlhood Diary.* Mahwah, NJ: Bridgewater, 42 pp.
　Wonderful exploration of Louisa's character as well as life in nineteenth-century New England. Grades 4–8.

Santrey, Laurence. (1986). *Louisa May Alcott: Young Writer.* Ill. by S. Speidel. Mahway, NJ: Troll, 47 pp.
　Ideal for poor readers. I used this as an example of how to write a biography for Author Expert Project. Grades 1–4.

Hans Christian Anderson

Garst, Shannon. (1965). *Hans Christian Anderson.* Boston: Houghton-Mifflin.

Frances Hodgson Burnett

Burnett, Frances Hodgson. (1980). *The One I Knew the Best of All: A Memory of the Mind of a Child.* New York: Ayer.
　Advanced readers and fans of *The Secret Garden* will enjoy this one. Try reading aloud excerpts for author study.

Carpenter, Angelica S., & Shirly, Jean. (1990). *Frances Hodgson Burnett: Beyond the Secret Garden.* Minneapolis: Lerner, 1990.
　A riveting story with photographs of the author.

Charles Dickens

Kyle, Elisabeth. (1966). *Great Ambitions: The Early Years of Charles Dickens.* New York: Holt. Grades 6–8.

Stanley, Diane, & Vennema, Peter. (1993). *Charles Dickens: The Man Who Had Great Expectations.* New York: Morrow, 1993.
　This simple text is beautifully illustrated. Grades 3–8.

Emily Dickenson

Longsworth, Polly. (1965). *Emily Dickinson: Her Letter to the World.* New York: Crowell. Grades 6–8.

Robert Frost

Bober, Natalie S. (1981). *A Restless Spirit: Story of Robert Frost.* New York: Antheneum. Grades 6–8.

Jack London

Garst, Shannon. (1944). *Jack London: The Pursuit of a Dream.* Englewood Cliffs: NJ: Messner.

Edgar Allan Poe

Anderson, Madelyn Klein. (1993). *Edgar Allan Poe: A Mystery.* New York: Watts.

A challenging account with an excellent bibliography. Works well as a reference book. Grades 7–12.

Stern, Philip Van Doren. (1973). *Edgar Allan Poe: Visitor from the Night Time.* New York: Crowell. Grades 5–8.

Harriet Beecher Stowe

Johnston, Johanna. (1977). *Harriet and the Runaway Book.* New York: Harper and Row.

Portrays Harriet Beecher Stowe's childhood and the events leading to her writing *Uncle Tom's Cabin.* Grades 5 and up.

J. R. R. Tolkien

Collins, David R. (1991). *J. R. R. Tolkien: Master of Fantasy.* Minneapolis: Lerner, 1991.

Easy reading with photographs and maps.

Mark Twain

Collins, David R. (1994). *Mark T-W-A-I-N.* Minneapolis: Carolrhoda.

A short, simple text that will appeal to fifth- and sixth-graders. Good also for older poor readers.

Greene, Carol. (1992). *Mark Twain: Author of Tom Sawyer.* Chicago: Children's Press.

Although this text is written for 6- to 9- year-olds, it is an excellent example of how to write for young readers. (See "Author Expert Choices" in Chapter 4.)

Meltzer, Milton. (1985). *Mark Twain: A Writer's Life.* New York: Watts. Grades 5–8.

E. B. White

Gherman, Beverly. (1992). *E. B. White: Some Writer.* New York: Atheneum, 126 pp. Grades 4–8.

An engaging biography that helps readers see parallels to the beloved characters and events in *Charlotte's Web.* The reference notes can be used to demonstrate how a biographer gathers information.

Walt Whitman

Reef, Catherine. (1995). *Walt Whitman.* New York: Clarion, 1995.

An eloquently written biography of a great American poet with particular emphasis on Whitman's writings concerning American ideals and the suffering brought on by the Civil War.

Padgett, Ron (Ed.). (1991). *Teachers & Writers Guide to Walt Whitman.* New York: Teachers & Writers Collaborative.

Laura Ingalls Wilder

Anderson, William. (1992). *Laura Ingalls Wilder: A Biography.* New York: Harper-Collins.

This story of Laura's childhood and adult life will be of most interest to *Little House* fans. Grades 4–8.

Anderson, William T. *Musical Memories of Laura Ingalls Wilder.* Available from Music For Little People. 1-800-727-2233.

In *The Little House on the Prairie,* after chores were done, there was nothing better than singing to Pa's merry fiddle music. These 13 family favorites include "Sweet By and By," "The Girl I Left Behind Me," "Buffalo Gals," and "Wait for the Wagon." The book has authentic Ingalls family photos, words and music to the songs, and fascinating commentary on pioneer life. 53 pages and 30-minute cassette.

Lasky, Kathryn, & Knight, Meriba. (1993). *Searching for Laura Ingalls: A Reader's Journey*. New York: Macmillan, 1993.
True pictorial account of a Boston family traveling to the midwestern prairies in search of Laura's home. This is a joint writing endeavor of a mother and young daughter. The photographs are great. Presents a unique and concrete way to study a favorite author of yesterday.

Little House Country: A Photo Guide to the Home Sites of Laura Ingalls Widler. (1989). Text by William T. Anderson. Photos by Leslie Kelly. Kansas City, MO: Terrell. 48 pp.
A full-color guidebook to homes and writing locales.

MacBride, Roger L. (Ed.). (1974). *West from Home: Letters of Laura Ingalls Wilder*. New York: Harper and Row. Grades 4–8.

Virginia Woolf

Lehmann, John. (1975). *Virginia Woolf and Her World*. New York: Harcourt, Brace, Jovanovich.
Challenging. Grades 8 and up.

Professional Resources

Ammon, Bette D., & Sherman, Gale, W. (1991). *Handbook for the Newbery Medal and Honor Books, 1980–1989*. Hagerston, MD: Alleyside.
An extensive guide for 36 books, including genre, theme, readability, author and illustrator information, plot summary, ideas for book talks and curriculums, and background information on the Newbery Medal and nomination process. Grades 4–8.

Commire, Ann. (1988). *Something about the Author* series. Detroit, MI: Gale Research.
A reference series that include pictures and biographical information.

Davidson, Tom. (1981). *Children Becoming Independent Readers: The Teacher Guide to Using Literature-Based Reading in the Classroom*. Hagerston, MD: Alleyside.
A good guide for the novice teacher or anyone who wants to implement an independent reading program for elementary grades.

Gallo, Donald, R. (Ed.). (1992). *Authors' Insights: Turning Teenagers into Readers & Writers*. Portsmouth, NH: Heinemann.
I can't say enough about this book. Twelve writers for young adults, including Robert Cormier and Sandy Asher, express their opinions on teaching literature and writing, motivating children to read, and classroom practices. The writing is lively, fresh, and inspiring. My favorite essay is "The Ice-Cream Syndrome" (aka Promoting Good Reading Habits) by Norma Fox Mazer. This books will either challenge or affirm your beliefs about teaching reading and writing to youngsters.

Goffstein, M. B. (1984). *A Writer*. New York: Harper/Zolotow.

Hansen, Jane. (1987). *When Writers Read*. Portsmouth, NH: Heinemann.
An valuable resource for teachers who want to use process writing approaches in connection with reading. A highly readable book with a wealth of examples from Hansen's classroom research as well as her own development as a writer, reader, and teacher.

Holtze, Sally, H. (1983). *The Fifth Book of Junior Authors*. Bronx, NY: Wilson.

Janeczko, Paul, B. (Ed.). (1990). *The Place My Words Are Looking For: What Poets Say about and Through Their Work*. New York: Bradbury.

Kingman, Lee (Ed.). (1986). *Newbery and Caldecott Medal Books 1976–1985.* Boston: The Horn Book.
Volume 5 in the series. The book includes the award acceptance papers, biographies, and illustrations.

Kirpatrick, Daniel (Ed.). (1978). *Twentieth Century Children's Writers.* New York: Macmillan.

Krumbein, Sue. (1985). *The Teenager's Bookshelf: How to Put Joy Back into Reading.* Palo Alto, CA: Dale Seymour.
A teacher's guide based on Sue Krumbein's success with junior high school English classes. Includes interesting ideas for book reporting, theme fiction lists, and popular young adult authors. Can be used with advanced fifth- and sixth-graders.

Landrum, Roger. (1979). *A Daydream I Had at Night: Teaching Children to Make Their Own Readers.* New York: Teachers & Writers.
A collection of engaging oral stories from children having trouble learning in school. The book outlines how to compile and produce student-generated books.

Lewis, Marguerite. (1986). *Hooked on Reading: 114 Wordsearch and Crossword Puzzles Based on the Newbery and Caldecott Books.* West Nyack, NY: Center for Applied Research in Education.

Lurie, Alison. (1990). *Don't Tell the Grown-ups: Subversive Children's Literature.* New York: Little, Brown.
This Pulitzer Prize–winning novelist examines the themes of the most popular children's books and describes the lives and worlds that created these loved stories.

Melton, David. (1986). *How to Capture Live Authors and Bring Them to Your Schools.* Kansas City, MO: Landmark Editions.

Moen, Christine Boardman. (1992). *Better Than Book Reports.* New York: Scholastic.

Murray, Donald. (1987). *Writing to Learn* (2nd ed.). New York: Holt.
An excellent guide for both student and teacher. *Writing to Learn* is one of the best books I have read on the teaching of writing by the process approach. Filled with examples and anecdotes from the author's own writing life, students are guided through a real writer's attempt to "make" a piece of writing. Five case histories of actual student papers include drafts, instructor comments, and student commentary on the evolution of their work. Murray's personal voice rings clear through this very readable book.

Peterson, Ralph, & Eeds, Maryann. (1990). *Grand Conversations: Literature Groups in Action.* New York: Scholastic.

"Presenting…" by Twayne Publishers' Young Adult Series. 70 Lincoln St. Boston MA 02111.
This extensive biographical series offers a critical analysis of an author's work, a comparison of each author's young adult novels, and a time line of events that influenced the author's writing.

Ress, David. (1980). *The Marble in the Water: Essays on Contemporary Writers of Fiction for Children and Young Adults.* Boston: The Horn Book.
This is 15 critical essays about the works of 18 English and American authors. David Rees, an award-wining British author, closely examines the structure, style, nuances, and language of popular authors for children.

Rollack, Barbara. (1988). *Black Authors and Illustrators of Children's Books: A Biographical Dictionary.* New York: Garland.

Short, Kathy Gnagey, & Pierce, Kathryn Mitchell (Eds.). (1990). *Talking about Books: Creating Literate Communities.* Portsmouth, NH: Heinemann.

Thum, Marcella. (1978). *Exploring Literary America.* New York: Antheum.

Trelease, Jim. (1989). *The New Read Aloud Handbook* New York: Penguin.
  The guru of reading aloud offers advice, guidelines, and a huge treasury of book profiles.

Weiner, Stephen. (1993). *Bring an Author to Your Library.* Hagerstown, MD: Alleyside.

Wollman-Bonilla, Julie. (1991). *Response Journals.* New York: Scholastic.

Zinsser, William (Ed.). (1989). *Worlds of Childhood: The Art and Craft of Writing for Children.* Boston: Houghton Mifflin.
  Six unique children's writers are profiled: Jean Fritz, Maurice Sendak, Jill Krementz, Jack Prelutsky, Rosemary Well, and Katherine Paterson. Each author comments on the sources of inspiration found in their own childhood.

Audiovisual Materials

American School Publishers, P.O. Box 5380, Chicago, IL 60680-5380. 800-843-8855.
  "Meet the Author Video Series." Live action videos features several authors such as—Ashley Bryan, Betsy Byars, Virginia Hamilton, and Scott O'Dell—sharing their lives, work, and writing techniques.

Creative Learning (Filmstrips and cassettes), Box 134 Saunderstown, RI 02874. 1-800-542-2468

- Newbery Author's Collection for Younger Readers:
  Meet Beverly Cleary

  Who's Dr. Seuss? Meet Ted Geisel

  Meet Stan and Jan Berenstain

  Meet Arnold Lobel

  The Man Who Invented Snoopy

  The Story of Beatrix Potter

  Meet Donald J. Sobol

  Meet E. B. White

- Profiles in Literature (Videocassette series).
  Sixty leading creators of children's books are interviewed. A brochure is available: (SASE) Jaqueline S. Weiss, 3023 DeKalb Blvd., Norristown, PA 19401.

Perfection Form Company, Logan, IA. 1-800-831-4190.

- Color-enriched author pictures, 8½ × 11, U.S. and world authors.

- Meet the Author (sound filmstrips—includes Paul Zindel, Mark Twain, Robert Louis Stevenson, Jack London, Ray Bradbury, Laura Ingalls Wilder, and several others). Recorded Books, Inc., 270 Skipjack Road, Prince Frederick, MD 20678. 1-800-638-1304
  Unabridged versions of critically acclaimed books masterfully narrated by professional actors. A few titles are narrated by the author, such as E. B. White, Robert Frost, and Langston Hughes. Gary Paulsen's books feature an introduction by the author and a follow-up interview. Available for purchase or rental. Informative catalogue.

Computer Software

The Amazing Writing Machine (Broderbund; for Macintosh/Windows. CD-ROM) Students can practice and learn about various writing forms such as letters, essays, poetry, and short stories. Offers 1,000 ready-to-print templates. Ages 8–12.

Storybook Weaver Deluxe (MECC, Macintosh/Windows. CD-ROM) Sophisticated and vivid graphics make this program an excellent choice for budding story illustrators. Its focus is more on developing ideas than writing skills. Ages 9–14.

Student Writing & Research Center (The Learning Company, Windows. CD-ROM) This easy-to-use program shows kids how to set up bibliographies, take research notes, and write reports. Ages 10–14.

Discovering Shakespeare (IVI Publishing, Macintosh/Windows. CD-ROM) Students will not experience the lushness of Shakespeare's writing, but they will enjoy browsing through this attractive guide to the author's life. Offers plot summaries of each play. Ages 10–15.

PrintMaster Gold CD Publishing Suite (MicroLogic. CD-ROM) This open-ended program offers endless possibilities for enhancing classroom publishing projects. All ages.

The Internet. The World Wide Web is a great source of new sites relating to children's literature, author interviews, author fan clubs, and book reviews. Several of the major publishers have web pages for young adult readers.

Quiz Answers

AUTHOR AWARENESS

1. (answers will vary)
2. Agatha Christie, Sir Arthur Conan Doyle, R. L. Stine, John Bellairs (and more)
3. E. B. White
4. Tom Sawyer and Huckleberry Finn
5. Madeleine L'Engle
6. (answers will vary) Arnold Lobel, Shel Silverstein, Eric Carl, Dr. Seuss
7. (answers will vary) Robert Frost, Emily Dickinson, Shel Silverstein
8. Beverly Cleary
9. (answers will vary) *The Giver, Bridge to Terabithia, Julie of the Wolves*
10. (answers will vary) Beverly Cleary, L. M. Montgomery
11. *Number the Stars, Johnny Tremain, So Far from the Bamboo Grove* (and more)
12. Beverly Cleary, Judy Blume, Mark Twain, Dr. Seuss (and more)
13. *Treasure Island, Dr. Jekyll & Mr. Hyde,* many poems
14. Louisa May Alcott
15. *The Wizard of Oz*

CLASSIC BEGINNINGS

1. *A Tale of Two Cities*
2. *Peter Pan*
3. *The Wind in the Willows*
4. *Mary Poppins*
5. *The Secret Garden*
6. *Stuart Little*
7. *The Wizard of Oz*
8. *Little Women*
9. *Alice through the Looking Glass*
10. *Charlotte's Web*

WHERE IN THE WORLD IS?

1. *The Lion, the Witch, and the Wardrobe*
2. *Heidi*
3. *Peter Pan*
4. *The Secret Garden*
5. *From the Mixed-Up Files...*
6. *The Book of Three*
7. *The Legends of King Arthur*

8. *Lord of the Rings*
9. *Mossflower*
10. *The Wizard of Oz*

CHARACTERS AND THEIR CREATORS

1. Eric Knight
2. Charles Schulz
3. Mary Shelley
4. William Shakespeare
5. Lewis Carroll
6. E. B. White
7. Robert McCloskey
8. Carolyn Keene
9. L. Frank Baum
10. Dr. Seuss
11. Sir Arthur Conan Doyle
12. Agatha Christie
13. Johanna Spyri
14. Beatrix Potter
15. J. R. R. Tolkien

Index